The Job, The Man, The Boss

Books by the Same Author

THE EMPLOYERS' MANUAL

THE SCIENCE OF CHARACTER
ANALYSIS BY THE
OBSERVATIONAL METHOD

Applicants at the door of an Employment Department. Every man a bundle of possibilities.

THE JOB, THE MAN,
THE BOSS

BY
KATHERINE M. H. BLACKFORD, M. D.
AND
ARTHUR NEWCOMB

ILLUSTRATED FROM PHOTOGRAPHS

GARDEN CITY   NEW YORK
DOUBLEDAY, PAGE & COMPANY
1914

Copyright, 1914, by
KATHERINE M. H. BLACKFORD, M. D.

*All rights reserved, including that of
translation into foreign languages,
including the Scandinavian*

ZUSAMMEN

PREFACE

The plan of employment set forth in this book is the outgrowth of fifteen years' experience in the practical work of advising men in regard to their vocations, counseling employers in the selection and assignment of employees, investigating industrial and commercial institutions for the purpose of professional advice upon efficiency in general, and increasing the efficiency of employees in particular, and in the installation, operation, and supervision of employment departments under the Blackford Employment Plan.

Our purposes in presenting the book are: first, to set forth the advantages of a definite plan and orderly methods of employment; second, to inspire all who work to study themselves with reference to their vocational fitness; third, to add our voices to those of many others in calling for more scientific vocational guidance of the young; fourth, to arouse interest among all thoughtful people, and especially among parents, employers, teachers, and workers, in the possibilities of character analysis by the observational method.

THE AUTHORS.

Hastings-on-Hudson, N. Y.
February 22, 1914.

CONTENTS

Introduction xiii

CHAPTER		PAGE
I.	Mind or Muscle — Which? . . .	3
II.	The Ideal in Employment . . .	10
III.	A Scientific Plan of Employment . .	28
IV.	Discipline	40
V.	The Job	62
VI.	Securing and Handling Applicants	76
VII.	Analyzing the Man — Heredity and Environment	104
VIII.	Analyzing the Man — Nine Fundamental Physical Variables . .	115
IX.	Analyzing the Man — Practical Application	181
X.	The Boss	200
XI.	The Employment Supervisor and His Staff	214
XII.	Some Functions of an Employment Department	225
XIII.	The Art of Handling Men . . .	240
XIV.	Educating Employees	249
XV.	Vocational Guidance	258

LIST OF ILLUSTRATIONS

Applicants at the door of an Employment Department
Frontispiece

                                                            FACING PAGE

Fig. 1. American Indian. Observe high nose and strong chin 136

Fig. 2. A Turkish Parade. Turks, evolved in cold, light northern Asia, are brunettes with convex noses 138

Fig. 3. A Group of Negro Boys. Note primitive forehead of boy in middle of rear line. Also flat noses and convex mouths and chins 140

Fig. 4. Filipino Girls. They have the characteristic concave foreheads and noses and convex mouths and chins of brunette races 142

Fig. 5. Chinese on Man of War. Note predominance of concave foreheads and noses, convex mouths and chins 144

Fig. 6. A splendid example of convex upper, concave lower, profile 146

Fig. 7. Savonarola. Extreme convex form of profile. Note especially convex mouth 148

Fig. 8. Kaiser Wilhelm II. Good example of pure convex form of profile. Note great energy indicated by nose 150

Fig. 9. An American Engineer. Pure convex form of profile. Note especially prominent brows . . . 152

LIST OF ILLUSTRATIONS

FACING PAGE

Fig. 10. Dr. T. Alex. Cairns, lecturer. Pure concave form of profile. Well known for good nature and humour 154

Fig. 11. Charles Dana Gibson. Pure plane form of profile 156

Fig. 12. A Study in Profiles. Beginning at the upper left, which is pure convex, the faces grade into plane at the lower left; then into pure concave at lower right 158

Fig. 13. Judge Ben B. Lindsey. A fine example of mental type. Observe triangular face . . . 160

Fig. 14. Hon. Wm. G. McAdoo. An example of the motive type 162

Fig. 15. Ex-President William H. Taft. A splendid example of the vital type, with judicial aptitudes . 164

Fig. 16. Henry Woodruff. An example of fine texture. 166

Fig. 17. Maxim Gorky. An example of coarse texture 168

Fig. 18. Theodore Roosevelt in early manhood . . 172

Fig. 19. Theodore Roosevelt in middle life. Observe changes in expression 173

Fig. 20. An example of fine texture. Concave mouth and chin 176

Fig. 21. C. F. Rumely. The first employment supervisor appointed under the Blackford Employment Plan 218

Fig. 22. Interviewing shop applicants at a big factory 80

Fig. 23. Interviewing applicant for an office position in a large organization 84

INTRODUCTION

WHEN a foreman discharges the best worker in his gang because of his own jealousy or ill-temper, or both, the loss to their common employer may run into thousands of dollars. If in the man so discharged there is an embryo general manager or advertising manager with ideas, the loss may run into the millions. Even when the man thrown out is an ordinary workman the loss is considerable. Production suffers, and perhaps machines stand idle until a successor is found. Other workers in the same gang, observing the injustice, decline in loyalty and efficiency. The best of them may leave. The foreman must spend some of his time securing a new man. It is an expense to substitute one man's name for another's on the pay-roll. In most cases there is a further loss of the foreman's time in training the new man for his work. Oftentimes the new man lacks experience or may be incompetent. There is a falling off in production, and work may be spoiled while he is learning. He may turn out to be utterly unfitted for the job, in which case he is discharged, and the whole vicious circle of loss begins over again.

Every employer who has considered this subject at all knows that he is paying out larger or smaller sums of money for which he receives no return because of just such occurrences, and every business man of foresight and imagination sees wealth slipping away from him because of the lack of men he needs to take advantage of opportunities.

Our aggregate economic loss from these and similar causes cannot of course be calculated. Some little light is thrown upon it, however, when we find that in one institution manufacturing agricultural implements, and employing, on the average, 2,400 men, 7,200 are employed every year. In a well-known steel mill 26,000 men pass annually through the institution in order to maintain an average working force of 8,000. The pay-rolls of a factory manufacturing electrical appliances show an average total of 20,000 employees, with aggregate changes in the personnel amounting to a complete turn-over every year. Perhaps one of the extremes is a foundry in the Middle West, with 1,200 employees, and 14,400 changes in the personnel every year. In other words, an employee's average length of service is only thirty days.

CONSERVATION BECOMING OUR IDEAL

This is one of the milder forms of waste in our industries. Strikes and lockouts, with their ac-

INTRODUCTION

companying disorder, destruction of life and property, and their paralyzing effect upon commerce and industry, have been, and are, a menacing drain upon our resources. The smouldering forms of antagonism and friction between employer and employee cost sums impossible even to estimate. Go where you will among employers of labour and you will hear a common complaint, a complaint that employees are inefficient. How serious and how almost universal this inefficiency is may be suspected from the astonishing increase in production, and decrease in cost, effected by scientific management and efficiency engineering.

The growth from a condition in which an employer worked side by side with his men, when they perhaps lived in his house and ate at his table, and he knew them and loved them almost as he did his own sons, to our present factory system, has been brought about by rapid strides after the comparatively recent invention of the steam engine. We have been forced by the necessities of the situation to devote our time, our energy, and our best and highest thought to developing machinery, equipment, and methods for the utilization of the vast resources placed in our hands by the invention of the steam engine, electric generators and motors, internal combustion engines, the turbine water-wheel, and by the results of exploration and discovery. It is only natural, under such conditions, that our attention should have been devoted to exploitation rather than conservation, and to the development of material forces and products rather than to the more subtle and more difficult tasks of conserving and developing our mental and psychical resources.

But the time has come when there must be a change. Conservation has become the industrial and commercial ideal. Instead of skimming the easily gathered wealth from the surface of our resources, and passing on to new fields, we are beginning to study scientifically how to develop our farms, our mines, our oil and gas wells, our orchards, our forests, and our fisheries, so as to make them permanent and increasing sources of wealth. Instead of wringing the last vestige of strength from our gasping men and women, and throwing them aside, we are beginning to ask how their mental and psychical forces, as well as their muscular strength and manual skill, may be developed and increased.

A PLAN FOR CONSERVING HUMAN VALUES

Evidences of the interest taken in this problem of human conservation are to be found in the formation of labour unions and employers' associations, in the rise of socialism, syndicalism, and

INTRODUCTION

other attempts to better conditions by moral or physical force, employers and employees working in opposition. A newer manifestation of interest is to be found in the vocational movement, in the efforts of our schools to change their methods so as to train boys and girls for the work in which they will be most successful, in the establishment of employment departments by many manufacturers, merchants, and others, in what is called welfare or social betterment work for employees, in corporation and industrial schools, and in many other ways.

Up to the present moment, agitation upon this subject has taken the form of destructive criticism of old methods. This was, of course, necessary. But perhaps we have reached the point where destructive criticism is no longer so much needed as the setting forth of a definite and practicable plan of employment to take the place of old methods.

It is because we believe that this time has come, and because of the insistent demand from many quarters for it, that we present in this book a plan of employment based upon scientific principles, a plan which is, and has been for some time, in successful operation.

The Job, The Man, The Boss

THE JOB, THE MAN, THE BOSS

CHAPTER I

MIND OR MUSCLE — WHICH?

ONE of the most common sights from our steamer as we ascended the Nile was the shadoof men. Hour after hour, day after day, under the burning Nubian sun, they dipped water from the Nile and poured it out upon the sands of the desert for irrigation. When the banks were high, one naked man stood in water up to his waist; a second was stationed halfway up the bank, and a third at the top. Thus, in perfect rhythm, chanting weird songs, they passed the life-giving, brown water from hand to hand.

In India we saw porters plodding along, mile after mile, with heavy burdens on their shoulders. On the Canton River in China we saw coolies on their treadmills, toiling day after day to furnish motive power for their clumsy boats. In the city of Canton we saw flour ground by great millstones turned by men who ran upon treadmills until they almost dropped with exhaustion.

And the wages paid to all of these men, some of them furnishing human muscle power in quantities of which we in America can scarcely conceive, average between 10 and 15 cents a day.

Cheap labour? Yes, perhaps it is cheap labour. But it is not cheap power. It is the most expensive and most wasteful form of motive power known. Even at 10 cents a day, and working at their highest possible muscular efficiency, men can not furnish motive power for less than about $3 per horsepower per day. A large steam or gasoline engine will furnish horsepower at the rate of from $6\frac{2}{3}$ cents to 66 cents a day. To purchase human muscle power is, therefore, not the purpose of employment.

The wise employer seeks to develop and secure for his business the highest and best physical and psychical forces of the men and women he employs. It is only within the last few years that we have begun to understand the purely psychological nature of business. Even yet we only dimly understand the great truth that materials, equipment, methods, money, and all the other tangible factors in our commerce and industry are but the visible counters in a game played solely by the invisible forces of mind and soul.

CONSTRUCTIVE AND DESTRUCTIVE MENTAL STATES

Walter Dill Scott says: "Success or failure in business is caused more by the mental attitude even than by mental capacities."* Dr. Wm. S. Sadler, Post-Graduate Medical School of Chicago, relates in his exhaustive work, "The Physiology of Faith and Fear," a multitude of incidents from his own practice, all demonstrating the destructive effects upon the human body of such emotions as fear, worry, anger, hate, grief, uncertainty, and discouragement. He shows that almost every known form of disease, in some cases at least, has been the result of destructive mental attitude. He also cites a large number of cases in which speedy and perfect restoration to health and vigour has followed the recovery of mental peace, courage, or happiness. Thus, mental attitudes in the human body may be either destructive or constructive. Either they tear down or build up the physical and mental powers. In a similar way, destructive and constructive mental forces either tear down or build up business institutions.

It is no secret to any careful observer that every place of business or manufacture has its own particular mental atmosphere or spirit. One does not need to be a psychic to sense the spirit of har-

*"Increasing Human Efficiency in Business," page 134.

mony, teamwork, enthusiasm, and happiness in any successful business. Nor is it difficult to feel the atmosphere of gloom, suspicion, irritation, petty jealousy, discord, or careless indifference in one which is on the road to failure.

We have studied many business concerns. In every one of them we have found the mental and moral character of the man or men who dominated it reflected and exaggerated in the rank and file. In one organization a man high in authority was an inveterate meddler and gossip. Not even the lowliest worker in the organization was safe from his curious, prying eyes and his inquisitive nose, and no one, either in the institution or outside, could escape the sting and defilement of his slanderous tongue. It was inevitable that this destructive spirit should permeate the entire organization, until almost every one in it was both backbiting and backbitten. No one could come into contact with this spirit without feeling demoralized, less self-respecting, less efficient, and less happy.

By a curious coincidence, at the same time we were studying this institution, we also made an investigation of the most successful corporation in its line of business in the United States. Here we found the vice-president, who was also its chief executive, and the twelve department heads associated with him, happy and harmonious. Every man enthusiastically told us that he belonged to the finest and best organization on earth, and was eager to praise the character and ability of every one of his associates. Not once in our interviews with any of them did we hear the time-worn and all-too-universal stab-in-the-back, "Yes, he's a mighty good fellow, but ——" All through the offices and works, and in our contact with employees of all grades, we found the same happy, harmonious spirit of teamwork. We were quite prepared for the information that this spirit, this constructive mental atmosphere, extended to the patrons of the institution and the public generally, and that, as a result, its profits and dividends were higher than those of any other corporation of its size in the country.

HAPPINESS AND LABOUR COST

William C. Redfield, in his book, "The New Industrial Day," pp. 120-1-2, says: "Given the scientific spirit in management, constant and careful study of operations and details of cost, modern buildings and equipment, proper arrangement of plant, and proper material, ample power, space, and light, a high wage rate means inevitably a low labour cost per unit of product and the minimum of labour cost. . . . A steadily decreasing labour cost per unit of product is not incov sistent with, but on the contrary is normal to, a coincident advance in the rate of pay for the work when accompanied by careful study of methods and equipment, as previously suggested. Conversely, low-priced labour nearly always is costly per unit produced, and usually is inconsistent with good tools, equipment, and large and fine product, else such labour would not be low-priced."

In a large factory manufacturing a food product of international reputation, $25,000 a year was added to the wages paid employees, and $17,000 a year additional was expended in betterments of their conditions, such as lunch-rooms, gymnasiums, night schools, and sanitation. This addition of $42,000 a year to the expenses of the company resulted, not in a decreased dividend, but in an increased dividend. As a further confirmation of this principle we have but to call attention of the reader to his own experiences, to the fact that he does more work and better work when happy and contented, when interested and enthusiastic, than when he is unhappy or indifferent.

We might multiply examples of the effect of destructive and constructive attitudes in executives and employees, but the truth is so well known that we should merely be demonstrating the obvious.

Since it is mental and psychical forces rather than muscle power that we are purchasing when we employ men and women, we should therefore seek mental and psychical power that is constructive and not destructive. Expressing the idea concretely, we want men and women who love their work, who find joy in doing it, and who, because of their happiness and psychical inspiration, give us the very finest products of their heads and hearts, and, therefore, of their hands.

The plan which we are to present in this book is designed to obtain and to conserve for the employer, the employee, and humanity in general the highest and best constructive thoughts and feelings of those employed according to its principles.

CHAPTER II

THE IDEAL IN EMPLOYMENT

WHEN Thomas A. Edison is bent on realizing one of his ideas, his absorption in his work exemplifies Emerson's dictum: "Nothing great was ever accomplished without enthusiasm. The way of life is wonderful — it is by abandonment." He shuts himself away from all interruption in his laboratory. He works for hours, oblivious of everything but his idea. Even the demands of his body for food and sleep do not rise above the threshold of consciousness.

Edison himself says that great achievement is a result, not of a great genius, but of just this kind of concentration in work. And, until the mediocre man has worked as has Edison, he cannot prove the contrary. Mr. Edison has results to prove the value of his way of working. Even our most expert statistician and mathematician would find it difficult to calculate the amount of material wealth this one worker has added to humanity's store. Of the unseen but higher values in culture, in knowledge, in the spreading of civilization, and

THE IDEAL IN EMPLOYMENT

in greater joy of living for millions of people, there are even greater results. Other men of the past and present, in every phase of activity, have demonstrated that Edison's utter abandonment to his task is the keynote of efficiency and achievement.

And right here, too, is the ideal in employment: To secure, cultivate, and maintain this spirit of absorption in the work of every man in the organization — and thus to develop, conserve, and utilize the mental and psychical forces of our latent and potential Edisons.

Each employee, even the lowliest and least skilled, can be as efficient and as happy in his task as is Edison in his, but only under similar conditions. Mr. Edison is doing work for which he is preëminently fitted. He shows his fitness by doing it supremely well. He has created an environment under which he works at his best. He sees the results of his efforts. He receives rewards commensurate with his efficiency.

THE EMPLOYER'S IDEAL

These, then, are the ideal conditions of employment:

That each worker should do work for which he is preëminently fitted;

That each should work in an environment in which he can do his best;

That each should be able to see and enjoy the results of his work;

That each worker should receive a reward commensurate with his efficiency.

Industry, like health, is normal. All healthy children, and even men, are active. Activity means growth and development. Inactivity means decay and death. The man who has no useful work to do will sometimes express himself in wrong-doing and crime, for he must do something industriously to live. Even our so-called idle rich and leisure classes are strenuously active in their attempts to amuse themselves.

When, therefore, a man hates his work, when he is dissatisfied and discontented in it, when his work arouses in him destructive thoughts and feelings rather than constructive, there is something wrong, something abnormal. He is trying to do work for which he is not fitted, or he is in the wrong environment, or under wrong management, or he is physically or mentally ill.

The remedy for all of this, as we have seen, is to give the man something to do which he can do well, and to fit his environment to his needs. In practice, of course, *this means the selection for each job in our organization of the one man out of all others who, by natural aptitudes, training, and experience, is best fitted to fill all the requirements*

THE IDEAL IN EMPLOYMENT 13

of that job, and suited to its environment and conditions.

In fitting a man to his environment perhaps the personal element in that environment is the most important. One of the first things we all want to know about any human relationship, whether it finds its expression in work, play, society, or politics, is the human atoms with whom we are to be commingled and compounded in that relationship. We may readily admit the universal brotherhood of man, but we also have to admit that there are some of our brothers and sisters with whom we do not make a very pleasant chemical combination.

Hydrogen and oxygen by themselves form water, one of the most beneficial and useful of all fluids, but combine sulphur with hydrogen and oxygen, in certain atomic proportions, and you have highly destructive sulphuric acid. In a similar way, we are happy and efficient when associated with some people, but unhappy and positively destructive when compelled to associate with others.

In the ideal organization all the human chemical combinations are made by the wise master chemist in such a way that every employee is associated with immediate and more remote superiors, who inspire him to give only constructive thoughts and feelings, and each executive supervises and directs the work of the kind of men and women from whom he can secure the best results.

We have spoken about selecting for every position the man who is best fitted for it, not only for the duties of that position, but for the environment and conditions attached to it. A most important corollary of this proposition is naturally this: In the ideal organization the environment and conditions attached to every position should be such that the man who will fit them is the best possible man for that work.

RATE OF PAY AND EFFICIENCY

For example, if it is desirable that a man should express in his work neatness, order, accuracy, cleanliness, and beauty, then a workshop or office which is neat, clean, orderly, and beautiful will suit the man best fitted for that work. The blacksmith shops of the Pittsburgh & Lake Erie Railway are called "white blacksmith shops." They are well lighted, well arranged, and constantly kept clean. Even the walls and ceilings are whitewashed and never allowed to become smoke-stained and soot-smeared. As a result there have been gathered in these shops men who take pride in their surroundings, and who are glad to do their best to keep them neat and clean. It follows, of course, that these men take pride in their work and do their best with it.

THE IDEAL IN EMPLOYMENT

It is an old saying that the workman is known by his tools. Frank A. Gilbreth, in his excellent book, "Motion Study," page 59, says: "The influence of the tools used upon the output is large. No workman can possibly comply with standard motions unless he has the standard tools." In the ideal organization all tools and equipment are most carefully selected and kept in condition to fit the needs and requirements of the most desirable workers.

There is no factor in the conditions of employment more important than that of the rate of pay, and there is none over which there has been more controversy. The time is already here, however, when the enlightened employer no longer quarrels with his workmen about their rate of pay. In conference with one of the most successful manufacturers in the city of Philadelphia we learned that, as the result of his scientific study of costs and their causes, he had increased the pay of his men from $2.50 and $3.50 a day to $6 a day and upward, the pay of some of the men reaching as high as $18 a day. These men perform the same operations on their new wages that they performed on their old, and yet this employer told us that his costs per unit of production had been greatly reduced since he began to pay his men better wages.

"As manufacturing establishments are improved

and humanized," says James H. Collins in the *Saturday Evening Post*, "it is becoming clearer and clearer that in buying labour quality counts first, just as it does in materials, and that price is really secondary. While governments collect statistics showing wages paid in different countries, and that the cheapest product is usually found where the most skilful employees earn the highest wages, the American manufacturer is arriving at the same truth through his own experience in the management of works and through his export connections. . . . The vital point about an employee is not how much he gets a day, nor how many hours he works, but how much he can do with a given machine. . . . Each improvement in the quality of the output cuts labour costs. . . . The actual money saving on the cost-sheets is only a part of the benefit; for a high-grade workman on a high-grade job facilitates deliveries, helps sales, and forwards the whole organization. A few dollars additional in his pay envelope may count so little that it would be worth the money to be certain he will turn up beside his machine every morning when the whistle blows."

The ideal, so far as wages and salaries are concerned, is not to fix a rate of pay for any particular job and then to find some man or woman (efficiency not specified) willing to accept that rate of pay,

THE IDEAL IN EMPLOYMENT

but rather to fix upon the standard requirements in aptitudes, training, experience, and consequent efficiency for that job, find some one who meets the requirements, and then pay him enough to secure his very best constructive thought.

HOURS OF LABOUR — PERIODS OF REST

Next to rate of pay probably the most difficult point of adjustment between employers and employees is that of hours of labour. It has been only natural, in the absence of exact knowledge on the subject, that the employer should conclude that the more hours his employees worked the more they would accomplish. It is also perfectly natural that the employees should respond to this attitude on the part of the employer by feeling that the fewer hours they worked for the same rate of pay the better off they were.

Little by little, hours of labour have been reduced from fourteen to twelve, from twelve to ten, and from ten to nine and eight. The results have been nothing short of astonishing to both parties in the controversy. Who could have predicted that a man would do more and better work in eight hours than he had done in fourteen? And yet that is exactly what has happened in hundreds of different industries and different factories on both sides of the Atlantic.

Will hours of labour be still further reduced? The question can be answered correctly only by the application of the new scientific spirit, the spirit which does not assume, as we formerly did, that a reduction in hours of labour means a reduction in output, but by careful experiment and the use of accurate records, carefully analyzed, ascertains the truth. The ideal in employment will be attained when every man works just that number of hours each day that will enable him to accomplish the maximum amount of the highest quality of work.

Scientific investigation has clearly shown that men and women do more and better work if given carefully ascertained periods of rest and relaxation during working hours. When a man works either his muscles or his brain, fatigue poisons are produced in his system more rapidly than they are eliminated. These fatigue poisons, as science has demonstrated, clog a man's mental and physical machinery, slowing up every process, dulling the senses, and robbing every effort of some of its reliability and accuracy. A certain period of absolute rest and relaxation relieves mental and physical tension and permits the processes of elimination to catch up and overtake the production of fatigue poisons. In ordinary physical work, into which the mind scarcely enters, men have been known to accomplish 400 per cent. more in a given number of hours with carefully worked-out intervals of rest and relaxation than when working continuously. In mental work the effect has often been found to be even greater. In the ideal organization, experts carefully standardize the proper intervals and periods of work and relaxation for every job, and the executives see that these intervals and periods are made effective.

RELATIONS WITH SUPERIOR

Some years ago we had occasion to study the efficiency of a number of accountants in a bank. Among them was a young man of twenty-two, well educated, with splendid natural talents as an accountant, intelligent, honest, industrious, ambitious to succeed. There seemed to be every reason why he should be efficient. The bank was well lighted, well ventilated, and in many other ways a delightful place to work. His rate of pay was fully satisfactory to him, and his companions were congenial. And yet he accomplished little, and that little was so poor that he was hardly "worth his salt." Furthermore, instead of improving, he was rapidly growing worse. A little investigation soon brought out the fact that the chief accountant, while most efficient himself, and while securing a high quantity and quality of work from most of the other employees, kept this particular young man in a constant state of terror and nervousness. The young man was of an exceedingly sensitive and responsive disposition, and would have accomplished wonders if his loyalty, love of achievement, and ambition had been appealed to. Instead, his chief had attempted to stimulate him by rather sharp rebuke and stinging criticism. It took a great deal of careful and painstaking instruction to the chief accountant about the disposition of his employee and the right way of handling him, but such efforts finally brought results. This bookkeeper, who had been almost worthless, became a valued employee in a few months under right methods of treatment.

It is well known to any one who will observe and think even a little that every man, woman, and child is a separate and distinct individual in all respects, and responds best to the kind of treatment best suited to his individuality. In the ideal organization, therefore, every employee is handled and managed, not according to the whims, prejudices, and pet theories of his superiors, but according to the needs of his own peculiar type.

HOPE OF PROMOTION

Among the fundamental principles of the universe is the law of growth. Of the laws applying peculiarly to sensate beings, this law of growth, the law of self-preservation, and the law of race-perpetuation constitute a fundamental trinity. No matter how low a man has fallen, no matter how hard the conditions under which he lives, no matter how great his privations or severe his trials, let him but feel that the law of growth is having its way with him, that he is progressing, that he has the right to hope, and he will have courage and strength for it all. But take away that hope, and no matter how pleasant and agreeable his surroundings and conditions, no matter how great his achievements, how high his attainments, or how many and valuable the things he possesses, he will look at life with the tragic eyes of despair. When there is no opportunity for advancement, for promotion, a man may work under the spur of necessity, but his work has in it nothing of that joyous abandon which arises from constructive thought and feeling, and results in efficiency.

In the ideal organization every man performs his part with the hope of a better to-morrow ever beckoning him on. The law of growth applies also to the feeling of the wise employer toward his employee.

When we studied the most successful organization of its kind in the United States, already mentioned in these pages, we found that every member of the executive staff had been a member of the organization for from fifteen to thirty-five years, and that every one of them had begun work in the organization as a boy. Each of them had developed along the lines of his talents and tastes until he had become the head of a great department.

Now, the development of an office boy into a general manager, of a stenographer into a purchasing agent, or of a clerk into an advertising manager, is not a matter of chance, but rather of education. Every factory, every store, every office is in the best and truest sense of the word a school. One of the finest things about work done by the right kind of man under the right conditions is the fact that work is an education. There is more true and valuable learning, more real and permanent development, in work under proper conditions than in any other kind of schooling.

In the industrial era just passed and now drawing to a close, it was to have been expected that employers, with their chief attention absorbed by questions relating to machines and methods, should neglect the greatest of all their assets — namely, the latent but easily developed mental and psychical forces of their employees. The men who, like Carnegie, have made their organizations schools in which masters and millionaires were trained, have stood out from all the rest by reason of their success.

THE IDEAL IN EMPLOYMENT

In order that work may educate a man he must know what he is doing and why he is doing it; he must be taught not only how to do things in the best, easiest, and quickest ways, but must be taught why he does them at all, and why he does them in the way pointed out. We have encountered thousands of workmen standing at their machines day after day, working on parts of commodities whose place and function in the whole they had never been taught. Since the blunder of some obscure employee may possibly lose a sale or estrange a valuable customer, why not teach that employee just what part he takes in producing the goods and services of the concern and just how his part of the work may affect the patron who pays his money for it?

THE SPIRIT OF THE HIVE

Men are naturally gregarious — they like to "belong." Many a man is far more eager for the success of his team, of his club, of his party, than he is for his own individual success. It is natural for men to devote themselves and all they possess — even their life's blood — to a leader, to a cause, or to their country. Men who are often apathetic and indifferent to their own interests will rise to heroic heights under such incentives. It is easy for the wise employer to appeal to this quality through right methods of education.

24 THE JOB, THE MAN, THE BOSS

Many stories are told vividly exemplifying this devotion of men to a leader. Perhaps none is more striking than this one from the History of Napoleon by Lockhart. A company of grenadiers, former soldiers of Napoleon, had been sent out to intercept his march when he was on his return from Elba. "Either party halted until Napoleon himself came up," says Lockhart. "He did not hesitate for a moment. He dismounted, and advanced alone; some paces behind him came a hundred of his guard with their arms reversed. There was perfect silence on all sides until he was within a few yards of the men. He then halted, threw open his surtout so as to show the star of the Legion of Honour, and exclaimed, 'If there be among you a soldier who desires to kill his general — his Emperor — let him do it now. Here I am.' The old cry of Vive l'Empereur burst instantaneously from every lip. Napoleon threw himself among them, and taking a veteran private, covered with chevrons and medals, by the whisker, said, 'Speak honestly, old Moustache, couldst thou have had the heart to kill thy Emperor?' The man dropped his ramrod into his piece to show that it was uncharged, and answered, 'Judge if I could have done thee much harm — all the rest are the same.'"

We have never worked with a more intensely

THE IDEAL IN EMPLOYMENT

loyal and self-forgetful band of men and women than the employees of a certain manufacturing concern with a rather remarkable history and strongly individual policies, traditions, and ideals. This spirit of loyalty was created and developed largely by educating the employees so that every one of them could, and did, talk eloquently and enthusiastically about the past triumphs of "our house," about its clear-headed, common-sense policies, about its traditions of high quality and excellent service, and about its splendid moral ideals.

THE EMPLOYEE'S IDEAL

In the ideal organization every employee is looked upon as a bundle of limitless latent possibilities, and his training and education are held to be of far more importance than the invention of new machinery, the discovery of new methods, or the opening of new markets. And this is reasonable. Some obscure employee, thus trained and educated, may invent more wonder-working machinery, discover more efficient methods, and open up wider and more profitable markets than any before dreamed. Even if no such brilliant star rises as the result of education, the increased efficiency, loyalty, and enthusiasm of the whole mass of employees lifted, be it ever so little, by education within the organization, has yielded results in scores of institutions that have come under our observation within the last few years far beyond any won by mechanical or commercial exploitation.

The ideal for every employee, therefore, is that he should be employed in that position which he is best fitted to fill, doing work which by natural aptitudes, training, and experience he is best qualified to do, and working under conditions of material environment — tools, rates of pay, hours of labour, and periods of rest, superintendence and management, future prospects, and education — that will develop and make useful to himself and his employer his best and finest latent abilities and capacities.

We have seen that the ideal for the organization is that each man in it shall be so selected, assigned, managed, and educated that he will express for the organization his highest and best constructive thoughts and feelings.

THE MUTUAL IDEAL — COÖPERATION

There is one more step. That is the *mutual ideal*. It is contained in the other two — and the other two are essentially one.

The mutual ideal is the ideal of coöperation. There is no antagonism between these ideals. The old fallacy that the boss must get just as

THE IDEAL IN EMPLOYMENT

much as possible out of the workman and pay just as little as possible, and that the workman must do just as little as he can and wring from the boss just as much pay as he can for what he does, and that, therefore, their interests are diametrically opposed, has been all but exploded. It was based upon ignorance, upon prejudice, and upon privately interested misrepresentation. The new scientific spirit, working side by side with the new spirit of a broader and deeper humanity, has demonstrated, and is demonstrating, the truth, that in no other union is there such great strength as in the union of those who are working together, creating wealth for themselves and serving humanity. This is the mutual, coöperative ideal in employment. And it is for the practical realization of this ideal that we have devised the plan whose principles and practical workings are described in this book.

CHAPTER III

A SCIENTIFIC PLAN OF EMPLOYMENT

IN A large printing plant we investigated we found the foreman of the press-room purchasing ink and paper and caring for the stores of these commodities. The foreman of the composing-room, in like manner, attended to the purchase of type, electrotypes, engravings, and other supplies for his department. He also had full charge of his stores. As might be expected, he made more than his salary in commissions. The foreman of the bindery purchased glue, cloth, leather, wire, thread, strawboard, and other such supplies, and also kept an eye on what he had on hand and issued it upon oral requests to the members of the binding-room force. We were not astonished to find the shipping clerk buying nails, marking ink, wrapping paper, twine, and sheet-iron straps; but we were amazed to find that the general manager himself purchased coal for the boilers and lubricating oil for the machinery. We had expected to find these duties delegated to the janitor. We found that a little print shop not far away, owned

A SCIENTIFIC PLAN

by a brother-in-law of the foreman of the press-room, had been running along for nearly two years with no expense for ink, and scarcely any for paper. Modern factory owners will be quite prepared for the statement that even the coal purchased by the general manager himself was purchased by the ton and that the general manager hadn't the ghost of an idea that there existed in the universe any such standards as British thermal units.

That was the old way and the crude way of purchasing. We found the next step above that in an electrical supply house. There all purchasing was concentrated in the hands of a purchasing agent and his staff. This purchasing agent was honest and capable. He had sharpened his wits and studied markets until his employers boasted of him that he could buy materials and equipment cheaper than any other man in the business. An investigation of this company's records, however, very quickly showed that, although they purchased more cheaply per ton, per gross, or per linear foot, according to the commodities, than any of their competitors, yet the item of cost charged up to material and equipment in their products was higher than that of any of their competitors. This seemed strange, but further investigation showed that a great deal of what was purchased so cheaply had to be thrown on the scrap-heap; that a ton of coal or of copper purchased in this way somehow or other did not yield as much heat or as many feet of salable wire as it should. Besides these losses, we discovered that there was considerable dissatisfaction among customers because of the poor quality of the product they bought. Too many consignments of goods were returned because unexpected flaws developed.

SCIENTIFIC METHODS IN BUSINESS

In the truly up-to-date purchasing department there is a due regard for prices. But the supreme consideration is quality. And when it comes to determining qualities, to finding just the best material or equipment for the purpose in view, there is no guesswork, there is no taking the word of some one else, there is no favouritism. The modern purchasing agent proceeds upon exact knowledge. In his laboratory he analyzes and tests materials and equipment with scientific accuracy. He also determines by the same methods what are the standard requirements of materials and equipment needed.

In the early days of our industries, inventions and improvements in machinery and methods were looked upon as dispensations of Divine Providence, as it were, so far as employers were concerned. If some inventive genius, either inside or outside of the organization, made a revolutionary

A SCIENTIFIC PLAN

discovery, well and good. They would do their best to avail themselves of it as quickly as did their competitors. If not, well, they and their competitors were on the same plane.

No modern factory is complete without its experimental and inventing department. The inventor is no longer either a starving genius in a garret or a lucky fellow who stumbles on a discovery, but a salaried man with whom inventing is a profession.

We have seen the same changes occur in selling, financing, accounting, producing, efficiency engineering, and other phases of manufacturing within the last few years. All this simply means that which had been left entirely to chance or delegated helter-skelter to minor executives who might or might not be competent — and certainly were not provided with time, money, and equipment for accuracy — has now been placed in the hands of a competent person, amply provided with all necessary means for supplanting haphazard, hit-or-miss, guesswork methods by orderly, accurate, and efficient procedure and exact knowledge.

ESSENTIALS OF THE BLACKFORD PLAN OF EMPLOYMENT

The plan of employment here presented has been designed to operate upon the same fundamental principles. The plan closely follows in its essentials the evolution of other recent phases of our industrial and commercial life. In practice the plan consists in concentrating authority and responsibility for all relations between employer and employee in an employment department under the direction and supervision of a specially selected and trained employment supervisor. Wherever we have installed the plan our first step has been to select and train with great care an employment supervisor, and to assist him in the organization of his staff and in the creation of an employment department.

The first duty of the employment department, after it has been organized, located in its offices, and completely equipped for work, is to relieve foremen, heads of departments, and other line officers of the responsibility and trouble of interviewing applicants, selecting employees, making transfers and adjustments, discharging employees, and all similar duties and obligations. Thus relieved, foremen and other executives are able to devote their entire time, thought, and energy to administration and management, and to the specific duties of their positions.

When this first step has been taken, the employment department finds itself responsible for the personnel of the organization, finds itself faced with the task of creating out of whatever human

A SCIENTIFIC PLAN

material is at hand and can be secured the ideal organization described in the preceding chapter.

The advantages to an institution, large or small, of an employment department, are many. So great is the superiority of a definite, scientific plan over unstandardized methods, with scattered responsibility, that only by widespread adoption of such a plan in many different kinds of business institutions can all of the advantages be known. We suggest here a few which have been demonstrated in our own experience.

UNIFORMITY OF POLICY AND METHODS

First. An efficient central employment department greatly facilitates the application of a *uniform policy* to all relationships between employees and management. It is far easier to instil ideals into the minds of an employment supervisor and his assistants, and to hold them responsible for the realization of those ideals, than it is to instruct and hold in line a number of minor executives, such as heads of departments, foremen, gang bosses, superintendents, chief clerks, head stenographers, etc. The management may have high ideals as to justice, mutual service, loyalty, obedience, or any other qualities. This plan affords an opportunity for the better realization of these ideals throughout the entire institution.

Second. In a central employment department it has been found possible to work out and adopt *uniform methods* of dealing with employees. By careful study and experimentation the most advantageous methods have been determined and, as the result of experience crystallized in records, have been perfected. There must be one best policy, one best set of ideals, and one best method of employment for every institution. It is only by the concentration of all matters pertaining to employment in one central department that these policies, these ideals, and these methods can be determined and applied.

Third. Every business enterprise has, or should have, its own definite *standards* of efficiency and of corresponding rates of compensation for its employees. It should also have standards as to physical condition, education, experience, moral character, and other qualifications, according to the nature of the business and the position occupied by the employee. With uniformity and concentration of responsibility, the maintenance of such standards is made less difficult. One very frequent cause of friction and ill-feeling between employers and employees is the inequality of policies, methods, and standards almost inevitable when every minor executive in the institution is a more or less absolute monarch in his own little realm so far as hiring, "firing," and promotion are concerned.

ECONOMY AND CONTROL

Fourth. It is a cardinal rule of efficiency that concentration of function wherever possible results in the elimination of waste, and therefore in *economy*. First of all, there is economy in the time of foremen, department heads, and other executives freed from the necessity of interviewing applicants. We have already referred to this. In some cases it amounts to a very considerable saving. We have also found that the adoption of this plan effects large savings in the number of employees placed on the pay-roll. A sympathetic foreman, chief clerk, or other executive is prone to hire more men than he needs when applicants are permitted to go to him with their pleas. In a case which recently came under our observation, an office manager, moved by the artistic hard-luck story of an ancient loafer and town character, gave him a job in the accounting department at a time when competent men who had served the company faithfully for years, who owned homes in the community, and were valued citizens, were laid off on account of depression consequent upon reorganization of the business.

It is a practice in many organizations for executives to keep their forces intact, even during temporary lulls, so that a resumption of activity may not find them short-handed. It is a common experience to see workers in one department of a factory or store rushed to the limit of endurance, working overtime, while the working force of another department loafs. In all such cases a central employment department acts as an accommodator, equalizing the pressure, withdrawing workers where they are not needed, transferring them to where they are needed, maintaining reserve lists of workers for all departments, and keeping in close touch not only with the needs of each department, but with applicants who stand ready to begin work upon short notice.

Fifth. The concentration in one department of all relationships with employees gives the management a small handle, easily grasped and with a big leverage, for the *control* of one of the most important and usually most troublesome factors in a business. In this department there are standardized, and therefore uniform, records not only of all employees, but of all phases of the employment situation. This means that there is always at hand reliable, accurate, and definite information. Does the management want a man with some special ability at a moment's notice? The employment department has long had its eye upon such a man, either employed in some capacity in the institution or upon its list of applicants. Is it desirable to know which one of a dozen minor executives is the most successful in handling men? A digest of the records in the employment department quickly gives the answer.

EMPLOYMENT BY EXPERTS.

Sixth. By the adoption of this plan we have been enabled to put all employment matters into the hands of those specially selected, educated, and trained for the work — in other words, to *avail ourselves of the services of experts in employment.* This also is in line with efficiency and scientific management methods. The efficiency engineer centres all responsibility for certain functions of the organization in the hands of experts called *staff officers*, such as purchasing agents, storekeepers, and chiefs of power and maintenance, lighting, belting, safety, sanitation, dispatching, scheduling, and other such departments. The scientific management expert centres responsibility for all these things in what are called *functional foremen*. The results in both systems are well known to those who have had experience with them or studied them. It all means taking responsibility out of the hands of those who may or may not be competent, and turning it over to those who are known to be expert.

BROAD SCOPE OF PLAN

Seventh. By the installation of an employment department *the scope of employment activity can very easily be greatly broadened.* For example, it would obviously be a great waste for the accounting, sales, collection, advertising, designing, and several other departments and divisions of a store, factory, office, or bank, each to send out a scout in search of desirable applicants. But employment supervisors frequently either go themselves or send some member of their staff on a scouting expedition, searching for needed employees for all departments of a business. A central employment department can attempt far more in the matter of records, files, advertising for help, analysis of positions, and analysis of men, than would be possible without such specialization of function. It is also possible for the employment department to organize and direct all of those activities, with reference to health, happiness, and loyalty of employees, commonly referred to as welfare work. This is especially true with reference to general and special education and training of employees.

Our records show that the average employee in the average institution represents a capitalized value of between $2,500 and $3,000 to his employer. It is the function of the employment department not only to protect that investment from depreciation and loss in every way possible, but even to develop and increase its value.

Thus centralizing employment activities is the external mechanism of our plan. But its distinctive and essential features lie rather in the scientific analysis of all factors of employment and action based upon these analyses, interpreted in the light of experience and common sense.

CHAPTER IV

DISCIPLINE

"WHY, your plan is impossible! If we take away from our executive heads the right to 'hire and fire,' they will lose control of their men. Most of them will walk out. They won't stand for it."

The air of finality with which the foregoing condemnation was delivered when we first proposed our plan to one employer might have utterly discouraged us. But we had heard many other high authorities declare that certain things were utterly impossible, and yet these very things had been done.

We had an idea, originating in a good many years' experience and study, that the average executive would be only too glad to be relieved of a responsibility which took time from the regular duties of his position, and which he did not feel particularly well qualified to perform. The average executive, whether head of a department or foreman of a gang, is a man of intelligence and common sense, a man who is willing to listen to reason, a man who is not so puffed up with a little brief authority that he is unwilling to relinquish this prerogative if by so doing he can greatly increase the harmony, efficiency, and output of the department for which he is responsible. We believed that the very incompetency — not at all his fault — of the average executive to "hire and fire" would be the strongest argument in his mind for turning it over to an expert.

The average executive is incompetent to select and assign or to discharge employees. If in the modern, scientifically managed institution the executive or foreman is considered to be, and acknowledges himself to be, incompetent to select raw materials and machinery, how can he reasonably be expected to select, assign, or throw out, human values which are so difficult of analysis that some of the critics who want to leave the responsibility to minor executives declare in the same breath that not even an expert can be trained to analyze and understand human nature? It is significant that no one who insists that department heads should select and discharge their own men has the temerity to maintain that they are competent to do it scientifically.

THE "HIRE AND FIRE" METHOD

The average executive is not expected to select employees fitted by aptitudes, character, training, and experience for the work they have to do. He is expected to select such men as he can secure — who are not absolutely debarred from the work by some deficiency that he can see with half an eye — and then to try them out. Unless they prove to be hopelessly incompetent, they are retained for a short time at least; otherwise they hear the ultimatum, "Go get your time!" It matters not, of course, that the man so discharged, while unsatisfactory in the eyes of this particular official, might have proved to be a treasure beyond price in some other department. He is "fired," and, by an unwritten law, when discharged from one department must not be hired by any other.

The injustice to the employee thus discharged is great. But the loss to the institution is far greater. Aside from the fact that an executive might thus discharge a possible Charles M. Schwab, it costs from twenty to one hundred dollars to put a man's name on the pay-roll and take it off again. A group of thirty sales managers, representing as many different lines of business, agreed that the average cost of selecting, training, and putting a salesman into the field is three hundred dollars.

We believed that another reason why foremen and executives would be glad to turn over to an efficient employment department the duties and

DISCIPLINE

responsibilities of hiring, promoting, transferring, and discharging was the consideration of time. In one institution where we installed an employment department the comptroller, a very busy man, told us that the new department was saving at least a full day of his time every week. As he drew a salary of $10,000 a year, there was an annual saving of between $1,600 and $1,700 in the time of this one man alone. Our investigations have proved that either the executive must devote so much time to employment matters as seriously to handicap him in his other duties, or else attend to them in so hurried and slipshod a fashion that they might better be left to an intelligent office boy.

But, supposing for the moment that your foremen, or buyers, or department heads are competent, that they know just the kind of employees they want, and know accurately how to tell this kind from the kind they do not want, they are in very little better case than we have pictured them, because they have no time, no equipment, and no assistance to secure efficient applicants from whom to select. The unusual gang-boss may occasionally find time and opportunity to go on a still hunt for a good man at night when he is off duty, or he may have certain private sources of information; but even *he* is not equipped for anything like a systematic search for men. The average foreman is obliged to select from the little crowd of unemployed at the gate of the factory. The average department head or executive must rely upon chance applicants ·or the heterogeneous crowd that answers advertisements, either in person or by letter.

Suppose, however, that in any organization all of the executive heads are unusual, that they have more or less effective although somewhat crude methods of hunting out good men. We have seen such enterprises. But the spectacle of thirty or forty men, each maintaining a little employment bureau of his own, with its attendant expenditures of time, energy, and money, was an example of duplication, yes, multiplication, of work that ought to have made the management gasp. The department heads and gang-bosses felt the sad wastefulness of the thing, and it was because we knew that they felt this that we believed our plan was not an impossibility.

WASTE OF UNSCIENTIFIC SELECTION

Since the foreman in a factory, the chief clerk in a bank or office, or the department manager in a store is confessedly incompetent to select men and women upon the basis of their fitness for their tasks, upon what basis may we expect him to make his selection? His own opinion is perhaps the least

DISCIPLINE

objectionable basis. Every man's opinion is but the expression of his personal bias — in other words, an utterly unscientific and unreliable quantity, liable to be turned this way and that by the most whimsical and inconsequential of considerations.

We once knew an executive responsible for the industrial lives of 800 men. "My good father told me when I was a boy," he used to say, "never to trust a redhead, and I never have had a redheaded man or woman in my employ!" And yet there were any number of positions in this man's organization in which men and women with red heads would have fitted with far greater efficiency than those who occupied them. Other manifestations of this same personal bias are seen in the selection of relatives, old friends, fellow townsmen, co-religionists, fellow members of lodges, clubs, and secret societies, and people of certain nationalities.

Many most desirable applicants are lost to the organization when there is no central employment department. They go to one or perhaps two departments and are told that they are not needed. And yet perhaps at that very time employees of their particular abilities are most sadly needed in some other department.

Many an executive, with honest intentions but wavering will-power, would be delighted to turn over all employment to some one else because of the constant temptation to graft. We have found foremen exacting a bribe from every man they placed upon their pay-rolls and further sums from every man they promoted or whose pay they raised. We have known foremen to maintain a number of dummy names on their pay-rolls and convey the contents of all these pay envelopes to their own pockets. We have known other minor executives, in institutions where such practices were going on, sorely tried and tempted in keeping their honour clear. For these reasons we believed that executive heads would be glad to have their employees selected and assigned scientifically by a department equipped for that work.

And, as a matter of fact, they were glad. The protests came, not from the men from whom the prerogative of hiring and firing had been taken, but from the management. Our experience has been no different from that of efficiency engineers and scientific management experts. The first objection of the management always is, "Our business is different." When that has been overcome, we are fully prepared for the next objection, and it invariably comes: "Our foremen and employees would never stand for it"; or "Our department heads would never give up their right to hire and fire." In the end, if anybody interferes with the harmonious working of the plan or balks at any

DISCIPLINE

of its provisions, it is always the management. The minor executives and the men in the ranks fall in with the plan easily enough, and within a very short time are working harmoniously under it and, almost without exception, are delighted with it.

DIFFICULTIES AND OBSTACLES

In one very large organization where we installed an employment department the offices were fitted up, the supervisor and his staff chosen, all necessary blanks and records printed and ready to use, before any one, except the management, knew anything about the contemplated new departure. Then all executives, heads of departments, and foremen were invited to attend a reception and meeting in the suite of offices that had been prepared. Everything possible was done to make the affair pleasant socially. At this gathering the plan was described, the blanks to be used were exhibited and explained, and complete instructions were given as to their use. Emphasis was laid upon the advantages of the plan to the foremen and heads of departments. The men were encouraged to ask questions, which were carefully answered. As a result of this meeting the hearty coöperation of a number of the foremen was immediately enlisted, and observation of the plan in its practical workings soon won over the recalcitrants.

In another large institution where a method somewhat similar to this was adopted, at the beginning the task of securing intelligent and enthusiastic coöperation from the heads of departments was not so easy. While most of them seemed to fall into line readily enough when the plan was presented to them, difficulties speedily developed when actual operation was begun. At first, either through inadvertence or in the hope of finding the new rules inoperative, department heads attempted to hire workers without recognizing the employment department. Inasmuch as they found it impossible to have the names of the new employees thus engaged placed on the pay-roll, they soon changed their tactics. They employed men and women and set them to work and then sent them to the employment department to apply for positions in which they had already been placed. By patience and kindness, combined with vigilance and firmness, the employment supervisor finally persuaded these executives that this method would not be permitted.

Their next move, therefore, was to send people whose names they desired to place upon the pay-roll, to the employment department with an enthusiastic recommendation. Investigation frequently showed that those thus recommended were either former employees who had left with a bad record, relatives, or personal friends of the department head, or, for some other reason, unemployable in the capacity recommended.

In some cases there was the most stubborn resistance to every attempt of the employment department to study conditions. This resistance was met with kindness and consideration but absolute firmness. The resulting investigation always showed that there were irregularities in the department which the head of it wished to conceal. Sometimes it would turn out that there were dummies on the pay-roll or that employees were paying their superior for their positions, increases, promotions, holidays, and other privileges.

There seemed to be an irresistible temptation on the part of some executives to transfer men from one department to another without consulting the employment department. These transfers sometimes included a change in the rate of pay, and otherwise entangled the records.

In some cases, when a rush of work was anticipated, executives would send requisitions for more men than they needed, not trusting the department to find enough workers for them.

It was difficult at first to prevail upon some of the heads of departments to take pains with their reports to the employment supervisor. Some were lazy, some were indifferent, some were ignorant, and some evidently held the whole plan in contempt.

For some time heads of departments continued to discharge their men, for no good reason, simply to show their authority, or because of a whim or loss of temper or personal bias or jealousy. At times men in the organization who were disgruntled attempted to foment a strike.

MEETING DIFFICULTIES

All of these difficulties and others were met, first of all, by having the employment department so well organized, and its finger so closely upon the pulse of the entire organization, that every attempted irregularity was quickly known. As soon as the evidence was all in hand, the department head responsible for the irregularity was called in. He was talked with kindly but firmly. It was assumed, as a general rule, that his departure from the plan was due, not to any rebelliousness on his part, but to a lack of thorough understanding, which was often true. Desiring to shield themselves from the charge of ignorance or stupidity, heads of departments usually exclaimed glibly: "Oh, yes, I understand how to use the plan." Investigation showed that in some cases where this

DISCIPLINE

claim was made they did not even understand how to fill out the simplest blank; so the whole plan was painstakingly explained to them from their point of view, not so much from the point of view of the organization. The effort of the employment supervisor was to show them how the plan would benefit them, how it would save them time, how it would bring to light their efficiency, how it would supply them with more efficient, more congenial, more loyal, and less troublesome help, how it would enable them to make a better and better showing for their departments. Not in the first interview always, nor in the second, but finally every department head either fell into line or, realizing that he was entirely out of harmony with the new spirit of the organization, voluntarily tendered his resignation.

Nor did the work of the employment supervisor end here. Occasional get-together meetings were held with the heads of departments. Difficulties and misunderstandings that had arisen were threshed out. Questions were answered. Experiences were related, and in a quiet way much was done to arouse and stimulate enthusiasm for the plan.

In addition to this, an expert from the employment department interviewed every superior and minor executive in the organization, sized him up, learned his preferences and peculiarities, diplomatically wheedled out of him his objections to the plan, if he had any, and sounded him for suggestions for its improvement. Much valuable information was obtained in this way, as well as some valuable hints for the improvement of the service.

RESULTS CONVINCE THE OBSTINATE

All of these methods were effective, and one by one most of the heads of departments accepted the innovation and worked gladly hand in hand with the employment department. It was inevitable in so large an organization as this one that some exceedingly hard-headed and conservative executives should resist to the bitter end. When, however, they began to see the actual results their attitude changed. They found that the efficiency of the workers furnished them by the employment department was of a much higher quality, on an average, than of the workmen they had been able to obtain by their own efforts. They found the expenses of their departments decreasing, and the production increasing. They found friction and trouble with employees decreasing, and in the end they were delighted, because they had more time for the real duties of their positions and were free from interruptions, since they did not need to interview applicants. With the exception, therefore, of a few who resigned because they felt themselves

DISCIPLINE 53

wholly out of harmony with the scientific spirit of the employment plan, every one of these heads of departments not only gave the employment supervisor his enthusiastic coöperation, but formed the habit of going to him for counsel and advice upon many matters pertaining to his subordinates.

The method just outlined is perhaps the best for the average large business. In smaller institutions it has been found advantageous to vary this method somewhat according to circumstances. In one smaller organization the foremen were interviewed individually by the employment supervisor, the whole plan being explained to them, and their coöperation requested. All but one of them was immediately convinced of the advantages to be derived and pledged their support. In the case of one who was skeptical, analysis of some of the men who were giving him trouble and other practical measures demonstrating the value of the idea finally won him over.

In still another organization, where there was splendid discipline and unusual loyalty, the employment department was installed by a simple order from headquarters, every foreman and head of department falling into line.

One comparatively small organization began its work with an employment department by having the heads of departments themselves first of all analyzed and readjusted. The employment expert advised several changes among these executives which worked out so advantageously that, after some little adjustment, they were willing to have the same method applied to their subordinates.

DISCIPLINE BY FEAR OF DISCHARGE

Employing men and women scientifically by a properly organized employment department is no easy task even under the best conditions. It is difficult — and sometimes impossible — when the management cannot resist the temptation to meddle. If the minor executives and employees are perfectly willing and agreeable, then some official higher up is quite likely to be sure that they are trying to shirk responsibility. It is usual for some one or more of the management to fear that heads of departments, foremen, or gang-bosses cannot maintain discipline unless they shake all day long over the heads of their employees the club of discharge. As a matter of fact, an intelligent and efficient executive keeps that club concealed and uses it not at all except in cases of dire emergency — then not for discipline's sake.

Civilization has advanced beyond that stage of development where fear is the strongest motive to excellence. A savage or a criminal may refrain from wrongdoing — except on the sly — because he is afraid. But an intelligent, efficient employee strives to excel and to conform with the regulations of the organization in which he finds himself because of higher motives than fear of discharge. It is true that there are a great many men, not only in the lower grades of employment, but unfortunately in the higher grades, who are deceitful, whose ambition is to get as much as possible for as little service as possible. It is true that many employees seem to have no higher ambition than to beat the boss in some way. But to hold over such men the threat of discharge will never make them honest, or desirous of doing their best. Its only effect is to make them more cunning and more deceitful. Furthermore, the dishonest, shirking employee is not the type employers desire.

In order to build up an ideal organization, an organization in which all of the workers express in their work their highest and best constructive thoughts and feelings, men and women must be selected who are honest and truthful and who respond to higher motives than fear of discharge. In any organization such a standard of character may be established for employees, and through an efficient employment department such employees may be selected, and the unintelligent, the unreliable, and the lazy rejected. That an organization has set up such standards soon becomes known, and only such men apply as are willing to meet the conditions.

MEN RESPOND TO HIGHER MOTIVES

In practice we readily detect those who are untruthful, for example. They are almost certain to tell us falsehoods when applying for work. When they do, we frequently reject their applications and tell them why they are rejected. The effect of this is often interesting. One young man who had lied to us returned and pleaded with us to permit him to make another application. "I will tell you the truth this time," he said. "I lied to you before." Even the lower grades of shop employees, men whose training oftentimes had not included instruction in truthfulness, men who could scarcely comprehend at first that there was anything wrong in lying, returned to us and asked to be permitted to tell the truth.

It has been found, not only in our experience, but in the experience of many employers and other investigators, that even the crudest and least hopeful of employees will respond to higher motives far more readily than to the destructive motive of fear. In every human being there is a sense of justice and fair-play. This can be ap-

DISCIPLINE

pealed to, first, by giving the fair deal; and second, by quiet suggestion on the part of superiors, of the employment supervisor or some of his staff. Again and again we have adjusted differences between superiors and their subordinates, between employee and employee, by a straightforward appeal to the spirit of fair-play. The men who heeded this appeal were always pleased with the results. They had played fair, and it added greatly to their self-respect. We have seen men who began their upward climb in the world through trying to live up to one little unselfish act of fair-play.

The employer who does not avail himself of the natural, healthy love of work in his men as a motive for excellence loses much. No matter what a man's vocation may be, his work has the spice of romance. Into every kind of work, no matter how lowly, can be introduced a desire for artistic excellence. We have seen shovellers taking great pride in their expertness with the shovel, in the distance they could throw and the way they could land the shovel-load, either in a small, compact pile, or scattered, as they chose. The right kind of treatment and attention by the right kind of immediate superior, and the right kind of management, will make almost any man love his work and take pride in doing it well. The motive of pride is one that can be appealed to in all men.

A SCHOOL FOR EXECUTIVES

A well-qualified employment supervisor teaches executives what motives will be found strongest in each of their men. On one occasion we were called in conference by an employer with reference to a young man in his advertising department. The employer told us that the young man was one of the most brilliant he had, an enthusiastic, conscientious, and tireless worker, whose brain teemed with original ideas. Suddenly, and inexplicably to his employer, the young man lost interest in his work and became sullen, irritable, and practically worthless. "I don't want to let him go," the employer said to us, "but unless he braces up he is worse than useless to me." As soon as we looked at the young man we saw that he was sensitive, proud, and keenly responsive. "Some way or other," we said to the employer, "you have humiliated that boy, you have hurt his pride. He will be useless to you until the wound is healed. Perhaps, if you know how he was hurt, you yourself can apply the salve." The employer then acknowledged to us that he had severely reprimanded the young man in the presence of his associates, and recalled that this was indeed the beginning of his trouble. At our suggestion, this young man was treated with greater courtesy, consideration, and justice. Occasionally, when he had so far forgotten his wounded pride as to manifest a little of his old-time excellence, his employer would give him a quiet word of commendation. The result was that within a few weeks he was doing better work than ever.

Hope of promotion, increase in wages, bonus for efficiency, and other forms of reward have been found far better aids in maintaining discipline than fear of discharge. Love of the game is strong in nearly every human being, and in many animals. It was the victorious broom at the top of the smokestack at the mill showing the largest production that caused the Carnegie company to outstrip all its competitors, both at home and abroad. It is significant that this appeal was made largely to men doing the very roughest and coarsest kind of work. Any gang of ditchdiggers will pitch in and make the dirt fly in order to outdistance another gang. It was this spirit of the game, introduced into the work at the Isthmus, that enabled Colonel Goethals and his men to make such remarkable records.

Finally, and perhaps the most potent of all means in an executive's hands for maintaining discipline, is the personal element. When you cannot get a man to do a thing because it is right and fair, when you cannot get a man to do a thing because he loves to do it, or because of his pride in it, when you cannot get a man to do a thing for pay or for promotion or to win a contest, you often can get him to do it because he likes you and wants to please you. It lies in human nature for men to follow a loved leader cheerfully and gladly through fire and water, and even to death.

In actual practice we have found that the most successful handlers of men use these means, rather than their right to discharge, in maintaining discipline. Even men who have been wont to shake the club over their employees' heads can usually be persuaded to appeal to higher motives than fear. In general, executives under the employment plan are more thoughtful, more careful, more considerate in their dealings with their men when given to understand that every efficient employee is an asset and not an expense, and that they are responsible to the firm for him. Every executive, high or low, is made to feel that his men have been carefully selected and accepted only after consultation with him, and that if they do not prove to be efficient he is answerable. Both department heads and management are made to realize that the executive who complains of inefficiency, carelessness, or insubordination among his men condemns himself. We find that when executives are thus made to feel responsible for every man under their supervision and direction they are more careful to give them the fair deal, to give them an opportunity to develop and improve, and to realize from them for the organization their greatest efficiency.

Just as every foreman, department head, or other executive must answer to his superior for the good condition, efficiency, and standard product of each of his machines, or the proper care and disposition of his stock and fixtures, so he must answer to the employment supervisor for the health, happiness, and efficiency of each of his men. The ideal is for the foreman or other executive to keep his men, not discharge them—an ideal which is held constantly before his mind, and which results in better discipline, fewer changes in personnel, and far greater efficiency.

CHAPTER V

THE JOB

AN ADVERTISING manager of our acquaintance told his president and general manager that he needed a new copy-writer. "We have added that new line of brass, copper, and silver specialties and there isn't a man in my department who has the ability to write the dope, even if he had the time, which none of them has."

"I have got just the man for you," exclaimed the general manager. "I met him on my trip to St. Paul and I never in my life saw a man better fitted for that job than this fellow. I'll wire for him to-night."

"But," objected the advertising manager, "what has he done? What is his experience? Whom has he been with?"

"Now, don't worry about that a minute. I haven't got time now to tell you all about him, but I'll wire for him, and I give you my word you will find him all right."

Two days later the newly acquired copy-writer arrived to take up his duties. He had given up his position as bookkeeper at $125 a month, and had left his wife and children to pack his household furniture and sell his house and lot. The man was thoroughly in earnest, seriously so in fact, and did his best; but his copy was stilted, archaic, dry as dust, and otherwise impossible. The advertising manager did his best to tell him what was expected of him. The ex-bookkeeper tried faithfully enough, but his attempts at the light, swift, easy, effective style of twentieth-century advertising would have been pitiable if they had not been ludicrous.

After the general manager's "find" had been in the office a week, the advertising manager said to his chief: "I thought you said that man from St. Paul was an ad writer, the best you had ever seen. Why, he never wrote an ad before in his life! As far as I can find out, he never wrote anything before he came here. What put it into your head that he was the man for this job, anyhow?"

"Why, I thought he would be a wonderful literary man. I found that he had read carefully every volume of Dickens, Shakespeare, and Macaulay."

IGNORANCE OF REQUIREMENTS OF JOBS

This true incident is a fair sample of the ignorance of the average employer regarding the requirements of the various jobs in his organization, and how to find men to fit them. Nor is the average foreman or department head much better. Until they have been instructed, such executives continually send us requisitions for quick, active, speedy men for positions requiring slow, plodding, painstaking accuracy; for careful, cautious men for positions which require a certain amount of daring; and for solid, conservative men for jobs where initiative, aggressiveness, and originality are the prime requirements.

We had a foreman in one place who used to send to us for accurate, methodical men and then rage when he got them because they were slow and deliberate. We were once asked to recommend for an important position a painstaking, reliable man in whom economy must be a prime requisite. We recommended such a man. Within two weeks he was returned to us with the complaint that he had not accomplished anything. A little investigation showed that the man had been expected to take hold of a badly managed department, tear it to pieces, and put it together again. It was an emergency case and the principal consideration was neither carefulness nor economy, but speed. And to make haste in work of that kind required a man with considerable willingness to take a chance.

As a general rule, an executive will naturally incline to men of his own type, whether they are best fitted for the work to be done or not. This is the reason why the "live wire" hustler, the aggressive, impatient, strenuous type of executive always seeks to fill his ranks with men as positive and reckless as himself; and why the quiet, good-natured, patient, plodding executive is often surrounded by men of similarly slow but certain gait.

It is very human for a foreman or head of department, having chosen his men with such ignorance of the requirements of the positions they are to fill, to blame the men and not himself when they turn out to be inefficient.

For years most sales managers thought that the ideal travelling salesman was a bluff, hearty, back-slapping, hard-drinking, gorgeously apparelled individual, and the type still sticks in our narrative and dramatic literature. Scientific analysis of the requirements of the salesman's function, however, has given us the modern salesman, the man who gives far more attention to building business than to getting business, and whose motto is "He profits most who serves best."

ANALYSIS THE BEST METHOD

Edison gave us the incandescent lamp with carbon filament, which was a great advance in artificial lighting over anything that had ever been devised before. But scientific analysis of the requirements of an incandescent lamp filament has given us the tungsten wire, producing a far more brilliant light of better quality and consuming less electricity.

There is only one common-sense, efficient way of filling a position, just as there is only one common-sense, efficient way of determining what material is to be used in a given place.

The man who selects the different metals, alloys, woods, leathers, and other materials for an automobile according to his own opinions and prejudices, with no engineering tests to determine the requirements of each part, would not build a machine in which you would care to trust yourself going at high speed.

The employer who leaves the selection of men and women, out of whom he builds his organization, to foremen who guess at the requirements, or decide upon them according to their own opinions or prejudices, does even worse, because a piece of misfit human material may do greater harm than a bit of cast-iron where vanadium steel is required.

Some employers, realizing the necessity for more careful selection, have standardized to a certain degree their more important positions. But every job is important. The office boy in affixing stamps on outgoing mail may put a two-cent stamp on a letter to a customer in Paris. When that customer has to pay six cents to get his letter out of the post office he is exasperated at the carelessness of the house.

Over and over in our commerce and industry we have exemplified the story that used to be told in verse form in our old readers, and that ended: "The kingdom was lost, and all for the want of a horseshoe nail."

FOUR FUNDAMENTAL REQUIREMENTS

Determining the standard requirements for any job by the employment supervisor and his staff involves consultation with heads of departments, foremen, chiefs of divisions, and superintendents, with efficiency or production engineers — if there are any in the plant — and with the workmen themselves. It also involves a careful, painstaking study of the most efficient men doing the particular kind of work in question. A preliminary rough analysis of any job is a comparatively easy matter. The complete analysis requires a scientific mind, and an intimate knowledge of the tasks to be performed.

If there are no efficiency or production engineers in the plant, the employment supervisor or some member of his staff provides himself with a stop-watch and learns how to make time and motion studies. While the very best of results have followed the detailed standardization of jobs, so little has been done in this respect in the average plant that even the roughest, most general analysis has proved highly profitable.

For example, at the very beginning of the work of an employment department, and before any detailed analyses of jobs can be made, we set up four fundamental standard qualifications, without a fair degree of which no one is considered for any position. These essentials are: (1) health, (2) intelligence, (3) honesty, and (4) industry. They are indispensable.

No man is permanently worth even floor space, light, and heat, to say nothing of wages, unless he has health.

Unless a man is intelligent he cannot be taught — he will not develop. He will not understand, and therefore cannot follow instructions. Even in the lowest kind of unskilled labour the unintelligent man costs too much for supervision to be a profitable investment, no matter how low his wages.

By honesty we mean reliability — general trustworthiness. A dishonest man cannot do honest work. He may seem to be wonderfully efficient in many ways, but work, like everything else a man does, is an expression of character, and a man cannot be dishonest in character and express honesty in his work. Somehow or other he will manifest his essential nature, and one crooked act on his part may wipe out all the profits possible on a dozen years of his best service.

It goes without saying, of course, that no matter how healthy or brilliant or how reliable a man may be, he is useless unless he does things, unless he expresses his powers in action.

METHOD OF ANALYZING JOBS

To make sure that every employee has these four qualifications is a long step in advance in the average institution. These four fundamental qualifications having been determined, we inquire more particularly:

Does the job require physical or mental work, or a combination of both? Is it an executive or subordinate position? Is it light or heavy work? Does it require mechanical ability, artistic ability, commercial ability, financial ability, or the ability to handle people successfully?

By a careful classification and correlation of all these qualifications and others, we have designed a suggestive chart which serves as a guide to the employment supervisor and his staff in standardizing positions. This chart appears on the following pages:

THE JOB

FUNDAMENTAL REQUIREMENTS:
- Health
- Intelligence
- Honesty
- Industry

Physical Requirements:

- Body Build
  - Tall
  - Short
  - Medium
  - Heavy
  - Light
  - Medium
- Texture
  - Fine
  - Medium
  - Coarse
- Consistency
  - Hard
  - Rigid
  - Elastic
  - Soft
  - Flexible
- Condition
  - Neatness
  - Cleanliness
  - Order
- Health
  - Circulation
  - Nutrition
  - Respiration
  - Muscular
  - Nervous
- Strength
  - Arms
  - Back
  - Hands and fingers
  - Legs

Physical Requirements:

- Endurance
  - Muscular
  - Temperature
  - Nervous
- Agility
  - Equilibrium
  - Speed of foot
  - Climbing
  - Quickness
- Activity
  - Slow
  - Rhythmical
  - Quick
  - Spasmodic
  - Sustained
  - Violent
  - Gentle
- Skill
  - Digital
  - Manual
  - Pedal
- Quality of Sense Perception
  - Visual
  - Aural
  - Tactile
  - Olfactory
  - Gustatory

THE JOB

Mental and Psychical Requirements
- Speculativeness
- Conservatism
- Sociability
- Constancy
- Aggressiveness
- Perseverance
- Originality
- Initiative
- Imitativeness
- Obedience
- Imagination
- Judgment
- Versatility
- Dependableness
- Optimism
- Caution
- Alertness
- Reasonableness
- Decisiveness
- Deliberation
- Quick thought
- Observation
- Responsibility
- Responsiveness
- Calmness
- Practicality
- Analytical ability
- Speed
- Patience
- Courage
- Carefulness
- Prudence
- Ideality
- Materialism
- Inventiveness
- Accuracy
- Concentration
- Resourcefulness
- Foresight
- Independence
- Docility
- Self-confidence
- Teachableness
- Artistic ability
- Mechanical ability

Mental and Psychical Requirements
- Financial ability
- Commercial ability
- Executive ability
- Judicial ability
- Scientific ability
- Mathematical ability
- Philosophic ability
- Literary ability
- Verbal expression
- Love of people
- Love of animals
- Love of plants
- Love of travel
- Understanding of human nature
- Honesty
- Justice
- Cheerfulness
- Courtesy
- Industry
- Loyalty
- Conscientiousness
- Domesticity
- Enthusiasm
- Tact
- Persistence
- Alacrity

The Job
- Is temporary
- Is permanent
- Requires experience
- Requires special training
- Requires technical education
- Requires general education
- Is in line of promotion
- Is not in line of promotion
- Is union
- Is non-union
- Is open
- Approximate rate of pay

In this list we do not attempt to cover the whole field of human qualities. Nor do we attempt to make a classification scientific from the point of view of the psychologist. The list presented here has been found adequate for our needs and the needs of our clients, but is capable of extension and improvement.

SOME SAMPLE ANALYSES

In analyzing any job with the use of this list, the process is simple. The job should be studied with the list in hand or in mind, and its requirements, as to each of the physical, mental, psychical, and other considerations mentioned in the list, should be studied and determined. As a concrete example, perhaps the reader will find it interesting to study his own job with this list before him.

Using this chart as a guide, the following are some of the analyses made:

Specialty Salesmen

Good digestion
Buoyant health
Cheerfulness
Enthusiasm
Optimism
Pleasing personality
Verbal expression
Courtesy
Tact

Love of people
Initiative
Persistence
Courage
Resourcefulness
Patience
Understanding of human nature

THE JOB

Retail Salesman

Cheerfulness
Courtesy
Tact
Patience
Pleasing personality

Obedience
Constancy Alacrity Alertness
Understanding of human nature

Screw Machine Hands

Mechanical ability
Muscular strength
Quickness
Accuracy
Steadiness

Ability to read blue-prints
Knowledge of micrometer
Ability to grind own tools
Ability to set up his own job

Truckers

Physical strength
Energy
Intelligence enough to read and write English

Dependableness
Good sense of location
Good memory

Lathe Hands (Turning crankshafts)

Ability to read blue-prints and use micrometer
Accuracy

Dependableness
Mechanical ability
Skill from long training

Crane Operators (15-ton electric crane)

Quick thought
Quick action
Keen observation
Quick perception
Decisiveness
Medium degree of carefulness
Ability to judge accurately
   Size
   Weight
   Distance

Good sense of locality
Good sense of direction
Some mechanical skill
Excellent eyesight
Steady nerves
Good muscular coördination
   Energy
Dependablenesss
Obedience

Note Teller

Medium build	Patience
Digital skill	Mathematical ability
Carefulness	Neatness
Prudence	Orderliness
Accuracy	System
Keen observation	Good memory
Concentration	Judgment

EXPERTNESS IN SELECTION

With these analyses before them, the assistants in the employment department soon become so expert that they quickly choose the best man for any particular job out of the available applicants.

In one employment department two of the assistants became expert in teamwork, as exemplified by the following incident. One morning there were requisitions from foremen for:

1 Man for assembly work	2 Labourers for casting yard
1 Boring mill hand	1 Engine lathe hand
1 Carpenter	1 Milling machine hand
2 Chippers	2 Bench moulders
1 Crane operator	1 Patternmaker
1 Drill press hand	2 Teamsters
1 Grinder	1 Toolmaker

Taking the list, one of the assistants stepped out into the lobby and, walking quickly through the hundred or more men gathered there, chose the men wanted, one by one.

As the men were chosen they went into the shop employment office, where they were met by the other assistant, who had a duplicate list. In every case the assistant in the office knew for which position each man had been chosen by his team-mate.

CHAPTER VI

SECURING AND HANDLING APPLICANTS

THERE is only one legitimate reason for putting any man on the pay-roll. That is not because he is a brother-in-law, or nephew, not because he is a Roman Catholic or a Protestant, not because he is a Scotchman or a German, not because he is a Mason or an Elk, not because he tells a hard-luck story or is an adept at flattery, not because he has a sheaf of letters of recommendation, not even because he has made a remarkable record in some other institution.

The only legitimate reason for hiring a man is that he possesses the standard qualifications for his job, and will be a good investment for his employer.

Many of those entrusted with the employing of help do not seem to understand that the company is investing money in every applicant from the first moment spent in considering his application. They do not seem to realize that the company must secure an adequate return from its investment in order to do a profitable business.

We have seen foremen and heads of departments

SECURING APPLICANTS

spend hours and days of time interviewing impossible applicants whom they had no intention of hiring. Why they did it is one of the things which, as the old comic song used to say, "cannot be explained," at least upon any basis that gives the recruiting officer credit for having common sense.

One of the most difficult problems of conscientious employers under the old method is to persuade foremen and heads of departments not to hire people simply because they are sorry for them.

FITNESS ONLY LEGITIMATE REASON FOR HIRING

It is an injustice, not only to the employer but to the employee, to give a man a job in which he cannot make a profit for the house. Even if the man is not eventually discharged, he is working under a severe handicap if he is trying to do work for which he is not fitted, and is also under a bad psychical strain, because if he is intelligent he must realize that he is to a certain extent an object of charity. It should therefore be deeply impressed upon the employment supervisor and his staff, and continually reiterated, that no person must be hired who is not a profitable investment. Let this become a guiding axiom of the department.

With the requirements of every department standardized, and with this axiom in mind, the employment department sets about its task of securing applicants, and from them selecting men to fit these requirements.

Just as the wise purchasing agent looks ahead and takes steps to keep a plentiful reserve of material and equipment always on hand, so the wise employment supervisor takes steps to provide against the day of emergencies. It is just as wasteful and inefficient to take chances on being able to pick up the right kind of employees to fill vacancies from day to day as it would be for a purchasing agent to purchase supplies and equipment for the factory in a hand-to-mouth fashion.

There are many ways of securing applicants, most of them good if used with discretion. One of the rather unexpected advantages of scientific employment methods has been the fact that ambitious workmen and executives of unusual ability have been attracted to organizations where employment is done scientifically. It is well known to observant employers and others that any organization which maintains a high standard of efficiency among its employees naturally attracts a high order of applicants.

Happy and loyal employees, with the interests of their employers at heart, frequently recommend candidates for employment whom they know to be desirable. Employment departments in different organizations sometimes help one another by an interchange of applicants.

Employment agencies are sometimes profitable sources of applicants if used with discrimination and discretion. They are especially valuable in securing applicants with the education and experience required.

ADVERTISING FOR APPLICANTS

One of the most common ways of securing applicants is by advertising. Properly used, this method is one of the best. But this involves not only a thorough understanding of the requirements, but also the ability to state them in such a way as to secure the type of applicants wanted. An advertising manager of our acquaintance, not altogether unknown to the public, once advertised for an understudy. His advertisement was so sensational and flamboyant, it went so wide of the mark in describing the qualities of the man he really wanted, that of the five hundred who responded not one was desirable for that particular job.

Whatever the method of securing applicants, the employment department never loses sight of the fact already stated, that there is only one legitimate reason for putting a man on the pay-roll — namely, fitness for the job.

Applications come into the employment department in two ways: by mail and in person.

In handling applications by mail the first move

BLANK NO. 1

Original

REQUISITION
Office
Factory
Store

No._____

EMPLOYMENT DEPARTMENT

Please employ for the_____Department

One_____for Position No.

Rate_____

To begin work, Date_____ 191

With these qualities:_____

To replace _____

          Transferred to Dept.
          No longer employed.
          Promoted in this Department.
          Returned to you.

To increase the forces.

   Permanent   _____
                                          Foreman*

   Temporary   _____
                                       Superintendent

Date_____191

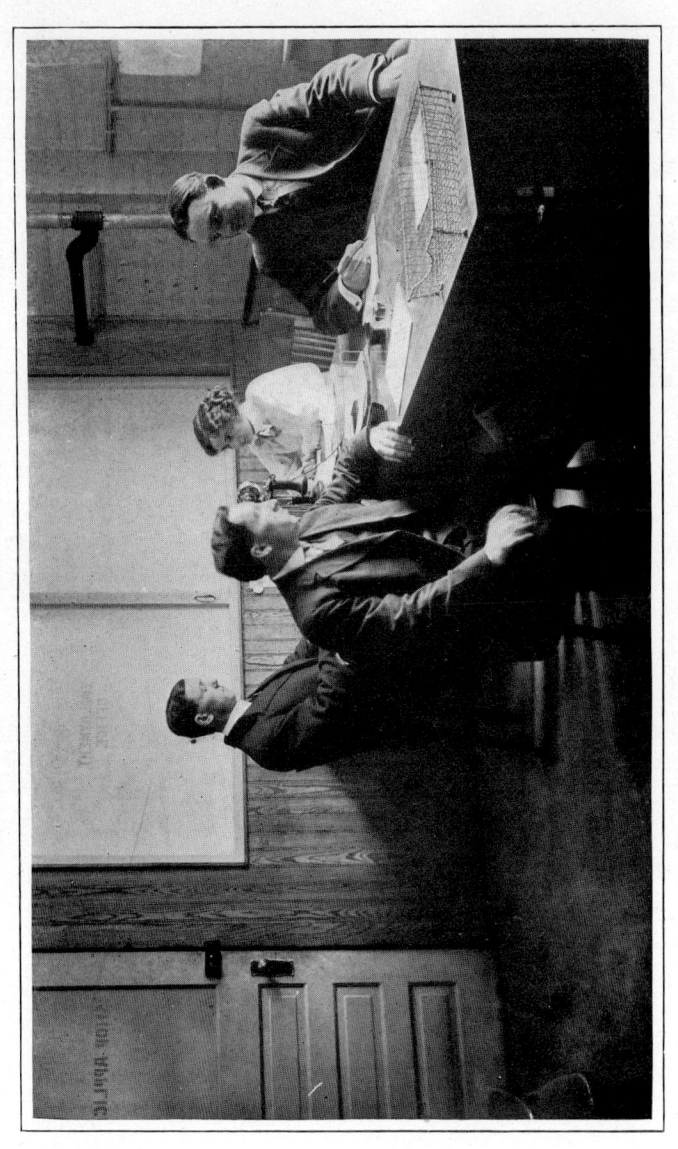

Fig. 22. Interviewing shop applicants at a big factory

is to weed out all that for any reason are on the face of them undesirable. A letter may show that the applicant has not had sufficient training or experience, that he is ignorant or illiterate, that he is careless and disorderly, that he is vain and boastful, that he is too well satisfied with himself to be teachable. If undesirable and uneradicable qualities are easily discernible in the letter, there is no use wasting any further time with the applicant, and if he has applied directly to the firm, and not to a keyed advertisement, he is courteously informed that his application cannot be considered. But should his application give reason to hope that he may be a valuable asset, he is requested to send photographs of himself and such other data as under the circumstances seem desirable. If the position to be filled is an important one, such applicants as are considered are asked to describe themselves as fully as possible, and to answer such questions as the employment supervisor may request.

It frequently happens that among those who are asked to send in more information about themselves a man is found who is clearly so well fitted for the position that he is engaged for it by mail; otherwise the most promising applicants are invited to call at the employment department in person.

BLANK NO. 2
APPLICATION FOR POSITION
(No person under sixteen years of age will be employed)

Name_____Telephone No._____

Address, Local_____City_____State_____

Nationality_____ Religion_____ What Union_____

Date of Birth; month_____day_____year_____Height_____Weight_____

If under 21 years of age, give father's name and address_____

Single or married?_____ How many dependent on you for support?_____

Ever employed here?_____ Under what foreman?_____ What Dept.?_____

Permanent?_____

Position wanted?_____Temporary?_____

When would your services be available?_____Salary expected?_____

Names of relatives employed here and their positions_____

Whom shall we notify in case of emergency? Name_____

Address_____

Please check the following list as accurately as possible as to whether you are:

Careful?	Careless?	Good Memory?	Forgetful?
Courteous?	Discourteous?	Obedient?	Disobedient?
Punctual?	Tardy?	Orderly?	Disorderly?
Accurate?	Inaccurate?	Cheerful?	Gloomy?
Industrious?	Lazy?	Patient?	Impatient?
Sober?	Intemperate?	Quick?	Slow?

PREVIOUS EMPLOYMENT AND REFERENCES

EMPLOYER	POSITION HELD	Give Exact Dates of Employment as to month and year	State Salary and Reasons for Leaving

In consideration of employment hereby sought, I represent and warrant my age and all above and herein contained statements true, and agree to at all times abide by and observe all notices, rules, and regulations of my employer.

Date_____ Signed_____

SECURING APPLICANTS

What foreign language do you speak or understand? _____

How much time have you lost by sickness during the last five years? _____

What was the nature of your illness? _____

In what places have you lived? _____
_____

What position do you now hold? _____

Why do you wish to leave? _____

What education and training have you had? General? _____
_____
_____

Technical? _____
_____
_____

In school what studies did you like best? _____

What least? _____

What do you read? _____ What kind of work do you like best? _____

If you could have any position you wished for, what would it be? _____
_____
_____

What if anything, are you doing to improve yourself? _____
_____

Can you manage people well? _____ State the evidence? _____
_____
_____
_____

HANDLING APPLICANTS IN PERSON

In dealing with all applicants in person the employment supervisor and his staff follow a definite procedure. Suppose for the moment that you are an applicant for a position in an organization where there is an employment department using this plan. If it is the busy season, you are quite likely to find the lobby or waiting-room comfortably filled with applicants waiting to see the employment supervisor or his assistants.

When your turn for an interview comes you are courteously greeted, given a comfortable chair facing the interviewer, and made to feel that you are in the presence of a friend who is just as desirous of doing his best for you as for his employer. You are engaged in pleasant, interesting conversation until you lose any self-consciousness you may have had when you entered the office, and are perfectly at ease. Then you are probably asked for what position you are an applicant, and the examiner discusses with you quietly your qualifications for the job. In due course of time, if this brief survey seems favourable, you are asked to fill out an application blank (see page 82).

During the time you are talking and filling out this blank, the interviewer is quietly and unobtrusively observing you and making mental notes of what he sees. He may or may not know your

Fig. 23. Interviewing an applicant for an office position in a large organization

name. He does not know what you are writing. But from external signs and indications which you cannot conceal he is learning something about your natural aptitudes, about your character, and about the use you have made of the talents with which nature has endowed you. In making these notes he uses Blank No. 3, Analysis (see page 86).

This blank is filled out in cipher so that it is unintelligible to any except the employment supervisor and his staff. In general, it is a complete but concise statement of your physical, mental, and psychical characteristics and aptitudes, your training and your experience.

When you have filled the face of your application blank, you turn it over to the interviewer, who talks with you about the questions on its reverse side (see page 83). These questions are so woven into the conversation between you and your interviewer that you do not have any feeling of being grilled or pumped. Your feeling is rather that you are being given an opportunity to state your qualifications, kindly counselled with regard to how your statements can be put in the most effective form, and advised how you can use your talents to your own highest advantage.

LETTERS AND REFERENCES

Perhaps you have brought letters of recommenda-

BLANK NO. 3
ANALYSIS

Name_____ Personal_____
Address_____ Photo_____

Colouring: Hair____ Form: Eyes____ Body: Texture____
Eyes____ Nose____ Motive____
Skin____ Mouth____ Mental____
Beard____ Chin____ Vital____
Condition____

Head: High____ Hand: Flexible—— Intellect: Capacity____
Low____ Rigid____
Long____ Hard____
Short____ Soft____
Narrow____ Short____ Type____
Wide____ Medium__
Square____ Long____
Round____

Energy _____ Vitality_____ Endurance_____
Health_____ Dress_____

CONCLUSIONS:

Positives   Negatives

_____   _____
_____   _____
_____   _____
_____   _____
_____   _____
_____   _____
_____   _____

RECOMMENDATIONS
_____
_____
_____
_____
_____

Date_____ (Signed)_____

tion with you. If so, you will find your interviewer courteous about them but not greatly interested. Of course, you believe that your letters are sincere, and your former employers and others have written truthfully about you. But the examiner knows by experience that the less efficient and less desirable an employee is the more eager is the average employer to get rid of him by giving him a hearty letter of recommendation to some one else.

We once knew a manager who practically wrecked one department of the business of a client of ours within the short space of three months. This manager had come to our client from a friend of his in the same line of business, bearing a most enthusiastic letter of recommendation.

"What on earth did you wish that man on me for?" demanded our client of his friend when he had cleared away the débris. "He did absolutely nothing while he was with me but spend money foolishly."

"He did the same for me," admitted the friend, with a grin, "but I thought maybe you could control him."

The finest collection of letters of recommendation we ever saw was in the hands of a futile old printer who had been discharged from every printing house of any repute in the Middle West.

Instead of letters of recommendation you may

Record of _____

DATE	FOREMAN	DEPT.	POSITION NUMBER	KIND OF WORK	DEPORT-MENT	SPECIAL ABILITY	EFF.	TOTAL PAY	REMARKS

SECURING APPLICANTS

give your interviewer references, asking him to write to your former employers, your banker, your pastor, and others. You are perfectly justified in making the offer, since these inquiries, with a promise to hold all correspondence strictly confidential, are very much in favour with some employers. But your interviewer will waste no time or postage in sending out any such inquiries. He is not interested in other people's opinion of you. He knows that the average employer, even if he were to state his honest convictions, would be guided by his own personal feelings and opinions or purely by guesswork, and not by reliable records of your performances. He would, therefore, far rather trust easily observable and infallibly dependable external signs of your character and habits than to take the word of a man who might or might not be sincere, and who, if he were sincere, might be utterly mistaken.

REQUISITION

Your qualifications being satisfactory to the interviewer, and there being a Requisition — Blank No. 1 (see page 80) — in his hands from some foreman[*] or head of department for an employee of your

[*] The word "foreman" is used in this and all other blanks here reproduced to designate the immediate superior of the applicant or employee. Naturally, in stores, offices, banks and other enterprises other designations will be used as circumstances require.

BLANK NO. 4

Original

REFERENCE TO FOREMAN

Mr._____ Clock No._____

to see Mr._____

Department_____ for position No._____

Rate_____ Began Work, Date_____ a. m.
p. m.

EMPLOYMENT DEPARTMENT

He is not satisfactory*

Reason why applicant is not satisfactory:

_____

_____

Signed_____
Foreman

*Note—If the applicant IS satisfactory, cross out the word "not."

Date_____ 191__

type, he carefully explains to you the nature of the position vacant, the rate of pay offered, the kind of work to be done, the general and special qualifications necessary for success in the position, the hours of labour, the rules, regulations, standards, and ideals under which you will perform your work, and, if advisable, the character of your superior, and how best to please him.

REFERENCE TO FOREMAN

If after this explanation you decide to accept the position, the examiner fills out Blank No. 4, Reference to Foreman (see page 90), places it in an unsealed envelope and sends you, with an usher if necessary, to the executive named. Since it is not the function of the employment department arbitrarily to employ, you are sent to the foreman or department head for mutual acquaintance and approval. If the executive finds you satisfactory, he shows you the place where you are to work, the desk or bench, appliances, equipment, and tools you are to use, and all of the other physical environment of the position offered you. In case this inspection proves satisfactory to you and to the executive, he notifies you when to report for duty, and returns Blank No. 4 to the employment department, properly filled out, when you have begun work. In case either you or the executive should

BLANK NO. 5

Original

NOTIFICATION
Office
Factory
Store

PAYMASTER'S DEPARTMENT:

Please { Enter on pay-roll
Change rate
Transfer
Pay off and remove from pay-roll

Name_____

Address_____

Position_____ Clock No._____

Department_____ Rate_____

To Position_____ New Clock No._____

To Department_____ New Rate_____

Effective (Date)_____ Hour_____ a. m.
p. m.

_____
Employment Supervisor

Date_____ 191__

SECURING APPLICANTS

not be satisfied with the arrangement, he returns the blank to the employment department as soon as possible, stating reasons. If you elect to return to the department for further consultation, you may be sent to some other executive — if there is a requisition on hand for some one of your aptitudes, training, and character. If there is no such requisition, your application blank and analysis are placed on file in the reserve list and you are communicated with as soon as a requisition fitting your case is received from a foreman or department head.

NOTIFICATION

Let us suppose that you are engaged and begin work. As soon as the employment department receives Blank No. 4, giving the rate of your pay and the time you began work, Blank No. 5, Notification (see page 92), is filled out and sent to the paymaster's department. You will observe that this blank is so arranged as to be used also in case you receive an increase or any other change in your rate of pay, are transferred to another position or department, or, for any reason, you resign or are discharged.

FOLDER

When once you have become an employee of the institution a folder (see page 94) is filled out for

NAME					CLOCK NO.				
APPLICATION	HIRED	DEPT.	POSITION	RATE	TRANSF'D	RATE CGD	PAID OFF	REASON	

you and placed in the Employees' File. In this folder are included all correspondence with you, all the blanks filled out with reference to your employment, and other memoranda of any kind that may be of value. In this folder, among other documents is the Analysis Blank, Form 3 (see page 86) filled out by the interviewer at the time of your original application.

RECORD

On the reverse of this blank is space for your record in the organization (see page 88). On this record, at stated times, according to the character of the business and the position you occupy, are entered data, giving essential information as to your efficiency and progress. How your efficiency will be calculated will depend upon the practice of the firm and the work you are doing. If a bonus system is in operation, your efficiency will be reported in percentages. If you are a salesman, your efficiency will be calculated in terms of sales, profits, collections, etc.

REPORT ON EMPLOYEE

Partly for the sake of keeping this record of your performance and partly for the purpose of keeping check upon foremen or department heads, Blank No. 6, Report on Employee (see page 96), is

BLANK NO. 6   Original

REPORT ON EMPLOYEE
Office
Factory
Store

Name_____

Clock No._____Dept._____Position No._____

Kind of work_____

Deportment_____

Special ability shown_____

POSITIVES SHOWN		NEGATIVES SHOWN	
Carefulness	Orderliness	Carelessness	Disorderliness
Punctuality	Cheerfulness	Tardiness	Gloominess
Accuracy	Patience	Inaccuracy	Impatience
Industry	Sobriety	Laziness	Intemperance
Good memory	Dependability	Forgetfulness	Undependability
Obedience	Quickness	Disobedience	Slowness

With reference to this man I recommend:_____

_____

_____

_____

Returned to you, Date_____ a. m. / p. m.

Reason _____

_____

_____

All tools, tool checks and other articles loaned No._____ have been returned.

Tool Stock Room No._____By _____
                                                     Storekeeper

                Signed_____
                                                     Foreman

Rate approved by_____
                                                     Superintendent

Date_____191__

used. This blank is filled out by the foreman and sent to the employment department whenever he desires to change your rate of pay, promote you or change your position in his department, transfer you to another department, accept your resignation, or end your service with him. The employment supervisor may call for such a report at any time, but, as already intimated, he does not rely wholly upon it in keeping the record shown on page 88. The data entered in this record are obtained by different methods, according to the character of the business and the system of rating employees in use.

This Report on Employee has been found to be of great value indirectly. When an executive is called upon to fill out such a report in connection with every change he desires to make in his department, and to state in definite terms his reasons for making the change, he uses more judgment and common sense and is less impulsive. Oftentimes foremen and other executives are either lazy, indifferent, or contemptuous, and therefore flippant in filling out these reports. A little experience, however, soon changes their mental attitude. One incident may illustrate this:

A foreman, being asked to send in Report on Employee for each man in his department, did so, with ninety-nine out of one hundred and four men checked as showing every one of the positives in the

BLANK NO. 7

RECOMMENDATION

Kindly fill out this blank with information about some one who you think would be desirable for us to employ.

Name_____

Address_____

Why is he desirable?_____

How do you know?_____

What kind of work can he do?_____

Is he now employed?_____ Where?_____

How old is he?_____What rate of pay would he expect?____

Married?_____Single?_____How many to support?____

Nationality?_____Religion?_____What union?_____

What is his relation to you?_____

Is he related to any member of your family?_____If so, what is the relationship?_____

Signed_____
Name

_____
Position

_____
Department

Date_____191__

list. Five only were checked with any negative, and each one of the five was reported as showing "gloominess." Within a week after these reports had been received, one of the men in this foreman's department came to the employment supervisor with a report on which every negative was checked, with immediate discharge recommended. The foreman was sent for, and his attention was called to the fact that he had sent in two reports on this man within a week; that in the first report the man was credited with having all the positives in the list and in the second was charged with being guilty of all the negatives in the list. While this one experience did not then and there make a new man of the foreman, it was the beginning of his reform, and within a few weeks he was taking care and pains in making his reports.

RECOMMENDATION

As has already been stated, loyal and happy employees frequently recommend for employment friends and acquaintances whom they know to be efficient. For their convenience they are supplied with Blank No. 7, Recommendation (see page 98). These recommendations are filled out and either handed or sent to the employment department, where they are acted upon according to the discretion of the supervisor.

Every time the employment department is called upon to deal with you in any important matter, your folder, with all its contents, is taken out of file and placed before the person who is handling the case. As you have seen, it contains, in compact form, all of the information in the hands of the department with reference to you and your relationship with the organization. Not only this, but in the folder is your analysis, made by some member of the department, and on the back of it your subsequent record. Here is an effective check upon the accuracy and reliability of analyses made in the department.

THE SPIRIT, NOT THE FORM, OF THE PLAN IMPORTANT

The blanks reproduced here are those used in a factory with several thousand employees. They are intended to be elastic enough in every respect to cover the handling of applicants and employees from the highest grade to the lowest. Their use, therefore, is not subject to rigid and ironclad rules, but to the common sense and good judgment of those who use them.

For example, in the use of Blank No. 2, Application, no intelligent interviewer would expect an ignorant man, perhaps unable to read, write, or speak the English language, applying for a temporary job as shoveller in the yard gang, to fill out all or even any of the spaces. Nor would there be any very extensive use of Blank No. 3, Analysis, in such a case. The higher the position to be filled, the more numerous and the more specific are the requirements, and the more completely and carefully are all of these blanks filled out. Necessarily, there are certain minor changes in detail in these blanks when they are used in other concerns. These changes will depend upon the character of the business, the policies and standards adopted by the management, and other considerations. The details are relatively unimportant. The spirit and purpose of the plan are all-important. In order that the reason and use of these blanks may be clearly understood, we summarize:

SUMMARY OF BLANKS

Blank No. 1, Requisition (see page 80), is an order upon the employment department by some executive in the organization for an employee to fill a certain position.

Blank No. 2, Application for Position (see page 82), is an application for position with spaces for the voluntary giving of certain information by the applicant. The reverse of this blank (see page 83) gives the interviewer suggestions for the examination of the applicant.

Blank No. 3, Analysis (see page 86), contains in cipher the complete and digested result of the observations made upon the applicant by the interviewer. The reverse of this blank (see page 88) is for a record of the applicant's performances after he has become an employee.

Blank No. 4, Reference to Foreman (see page 90), serves a double purpose. It is a letter of introduction presenting an applicant accepted by the employment department to the superior executive to whom he is recommended for employment. It also serves to carry the report of the executive upon the result of the applicant's call.

Blank No. 5, Notification (see page 92), notifies the paymaster's department of the hiring of a new employee or any change in rate, transfer, promotion, or removal of an employee.

Blank No. 6, Report on Employee (see page 96), serves several purposes: gives an executive's report upon an employee; recommends an increase in pay, promotion, transfer, or removal of an employee; gives reason for such action, and definitely closes the relations of the employee with the institution's tool, stock, or supply department; also serves as a check upon doings of executives.

Blank No. 7, Recommendation (see page 98), gives an opportunity for employees to notify the organization of desirable candidates for positions.

SECURING APPLICANTS

In a very small organization not all of these blanks are necessary. In a very large organization where there are many complications of relationship with employees, perhaps other blanks may be needed. "The letter killeth; the spirit maketh alive."

CHAPTER VII

ANALYZING THE MAN
HEREDITY AND ENVIRONMENT

WHEN a man suffers from tonsillitis he has an infection and inflammation of a part of the throat whose reason for existence was until recently a mystery. He can derive a certain amount of interest, if not consolation, from the fact that he inherited his troublesome tonsils from remote ancestors. Ages ago his forebears swam in the warm, salt waters of the young earth. Naturally, they were equipped with gills. These old worthies transmitted their gills to him, but in being handed down from generation to generation the legacy has been so modified by conditions that all he has left of it are his ears, Eustachian tubes, and these inflammable tonsils. This same man, when a schoolboy, probably braved drowning and suffered many a whipping because of his love for the old swimming hole. Perhaps this trait of his character was also an inheritance from his remote aquatic ancestors.

The researches of science into the evolution of

man — and of each part and organ of his body — have resulted in a far better understanding of his anatomy and physiology. In a similar way, a study of the evolution of the human mind and its activities has given us a far better understanding than ever before of human psychology.

Just as the tonsils, the Eustachian tubes, and the ears in present-day man are relics of gills, so there are in every other part of the body interesting and significant relics of other stages in the evolution of the race. Just as the passion of the average small boy for the water is perhaps an inheritance from ancestors whose home was in the sea, so innumerable other traits in human beings as we know them to-day are inheritances from ancestors of cruder forms.

According to the law of the survival of the fittest, individuals having physical and mental traits enabling them to live with the greatest degree of adaptation to their environment, tend to survive longest, and therefore to reproduce themselves in the largest number of offspring inheriting these same physical and mental traits.

EVOLUTION OF PHYSICAL AND PSYCHICAL TRAITS

The prehistoric antelope, whose ears could detect the slightest movement in the underbrush, heard the tiger crouching for a spring and fled.

He became the parent of offspring who inherited his excellent hearing. The antelope whose hearing was duller failed to hear the approach of his enemy, and perished before mating. Thus was evolved the keenly sensitive hearing of the antelope.

Since these same selective processes operated in the evolution of man, it has come about that every bone, every muscle, every nerve, every feature of the body, as well as the general physical conformation, colour, texture, and consistency, are the result of this ages-long process of selection and survival.

This law of the survival of the fittest applies also to the survival of mental and physical traits. For example, in a certain environment that individual who had the greatest courage would survive and reproduce courageous offspring. In another environment that individual who had the greatest caution would survive and transmit his cautious soul to his posterity. And so each of our intellectual and emotional characteristics is the result of this same process of variation, selection, and survival, covering a period of unknown ages.

In short, there is no aptitude, trait, or characteristic in man which is accidental. The size, shape, proportion, colour, texture, consistency, and condition of every part, every organ, every feature of his body, as well as every little twist and turn of his

ANALYZING THE MAN

mental abilities, his morals, and his disposition, are the result of heredity and environment of his ancestors extending back into antiquity for uncounted ages, plus his own environment and experiences. The significant truth in this is that *both physical* and *psychical* natures of man are the result of this process of evolution, and that the evolution of one has been *coincident* and *synchronous* with the evolution of the other.

MUTUAL AND RECIPROCAL INFLUENCE OF BODY AND MIND

A few other facts, taken in connection with this one, are also important. The intimate relation between thought and feeling and the body is well known to every one who has given his own experiences a moment's consideration. From the standpoint of science this relationship is so marked that there are many careful investigators who hold to the theory that both thought and feeling are merely physical states and activities. Whether we accept this extreme view or not, we must agree with the more moderate statement that every mental and psychical state and activity is accompanied by its particular physical reaction.

Prof. George Trumbull Ladd, of Yale, says: "All facts too obviously impress upon us the conclusion, how pervasive, intimate, varied, and profound are the mutual relations — the correlations — of the physical mechanism and the phenomena of consciousness."*

This is especially true of the emotions. So marked are the physical accompaniments of emotion that many different forms of emotion can be either induced, aggravated, or subdued by voluntary production or inhibition of their accompanying physical states and activities. Says Prof. William James: "The general causes of the emotions are indubitably physiological."†

We therefore have the physical and the mental and psychical evolution of man not only progressing hand in hand over many centuries, but *profoundly affecting each other* every step of the way. Every thought has its accompanying vibration in the brain cells. Every emotion, however faint and transient, has its expression in some kind of muscular action and organic reaction. Prevailing modes and directions of thought have given permanent arrangement and development to the brain cells and to other parts of the body. Prevailing states of emotion have actually built up or torn down certain parts of the body, and have given permanent form and expression to other parts. Certain thoughts and feelings have operated to

*Elements of Physiological Psychology, page 582.
†The Principles of Psychology, Vol. II, page 448.

take men into certain kinds of environment. These different kinds of environment, in their turn, have left their indelible marks upon the body, the minds, and hearts of all who dwelt and worked in their midst. For example, thoughts and feelings of weariness with routine, of aggressiveness and courage, of longing for new scenes, new achievements, have in all the ages driven both animals and men into the frontiers of their habitable worlds. Furthermore, frontier life, with its activities, its hardships, its perils, its peculiar forms of nourishment, clothing, and shelter, has had its effect not only upon the mental and psychical characteristics of animals and men, but upon their physical structure and appearance.

THEORY OF PSYCHOPHYSICAL CORRESPONDENCE

On the other hand, feelings of prudence, love of routine, established customs, attachment to familiar scenes and familiar faces, love of ease, love of comfort, certainty of nourishment and shelter no matter how meagre, have influenced both animals and men to remain in the serene, protected, salubrious, mild environment of the cradles of life. In turn, this environment has reacted upon them and has left the indelible traces of its influence not only upon their characters but upon their bodies. Many other examples of similar import might be cited in support of the theory that *there is a constant correspondence between the mental and psychical characteristics of any individual and his physical characteristics.*

This theory is stated by Prof. J. Mark Baldwin in "Development and Evolution," pages 25, 26, 29, as follows: "Furthermore, we may say that no physical character which has mental correlations is completely understood until these latter are exhaustively determined, and also that no mental character escapes physical correlation. Recent research in the psychological and physiological laboratories is establishing many such psychophysical correlations: that of emotion with motor processes; of attention, rhythm, and the time sense with vasomotor changes; that of mental work with nervous fatigue, etc., through all the main problems of this department. All this affords, in so far, at once illustration and proof of the general formula of psychophysical parallelism. . . . It has been the psychophysical, not the physical alone nor the mental alone, which has been the unit of selection in the main trend of evolution, and Nature has done what we are now urging the science of evolution to do — she has carried forward the two series together, thus producing a single genetic movement. . . . The fact of correlated variation, moreover, is to be carried

ANALYZING THE MAN

over to the relation between organic and mental variations *in different individuals*. Many instances are known which prove it; that they are not more numerous is due, I think, to the neglect of recognition of it in seeking genetic explanations." This theory is now almost universally accepted by scientists, but in many different modifications, with reference to its form and extent.

EARLY ATTEMPTS AT CHARACTER INTERPRETATION

Thinkers and investigators of very early times either assumed or suspected the truth of psychophysical correspondence. It was because of this assumption or belief in the correspondence between character and physical appearance that men began to try to read the character of their fellows in their faces, heads, hands, and bodies generally, from the earliest times known to history. That one's occupation stamps its impress on the outward expression was observed and recorded by an Egyptian scribe of the twelfth dynasty, about 2600 B. C. This papyrus is now in the British Museum. Aristotle was a devoted student of physiognomy and compared the features and dispositions of men and animals 350 B. C. Hippocrates, known as the Father of Medicine, 460 B. C., refers to the influence of environment in determining disposition, and of the reaction of these on the features. Classic literature from Homer down to the present time is full of expressions indicating at least a partial acceptance of this theory.

The high brows and lean cheeks of the thinker and scholar; the high, large nose of courage and aggressiveness; the thick neck and fleshy lips of sensuality; the thin lips and cold eye of cruelty; the round face and full figure of good nature; the dark eyes, hair, and skin of revenge; the keen, sharp face of the scold; and the broad, flat face of phlegmatism are as familiar in literature as they are in everyday life.

SIFTING THE EVIDENCE — VERIFYING TRUTH

Ever since these early days there have been attempts at character reading. Many different avenues of approach to the subject have been opened up: some by sincere and earnest men of scientific minds and scholarly attainments; some by sincere and earnest but unscientific laymen; and some by mountebanks and charlatans. As the result of all this study, research, and empiricism, a great mass of alleged facts about physical characteristics in man and their corresponding mental and psychical characteristics has accumulated. When we began our research more than fifteen years ago, we found a very considerable library covering every phase of character interpretation, both scientific and unscientific. A great deal has been added since that time. Much of this literature is pseudo-scientific, and some of it is pure quackery. But careful and detailed observations upon more than 12,000 individuals, with the use of exact measurements and uniform records, have demonstrated conclusively that many of the conclusions of early workers in this difficult field are substantially correct. This investigation has established many other definite psychophysical correspondences. All of these correspondences, still further verified by observations in groups upon more than one hundred thousand individuals in the United States and eighteen foreign countries, correlated, classified, and reduced to a comparatively few laws, form a scientific basis for the analysis of men to determine their fitness for their work and environment.

In the very nature of the case, this science of character analysis by the observational method cannot be a science in the same sense in which chemistry and mathematics are sciences. So far our studies and experiences do not lead us to expect that it ever can become absolute and exact. Human nature is complicated by too many variables and obscured by too much that is elusive and intangible. We cannot put a man on the scales and determine that he has so many milligrams of common sense or apply the micrometer to him and say that he has so many millimetres of financial ability. Human traits and human values are relative and can be determined and stated only relatively.

On the other hand, inasmuch as it is organized and classified knowledge, the system of character analysis upon which judgment of the man in our employment plan is based is entitled to be called a science. It is a science in the same sense in which horticulture, agriculture, etc., are sciences. While the knowledge upon which it is based can never be mathematically exact, it is fundamentally sound from the standpoint of evolution, heredity, environment, biology, physiology, and psychology, and has been verified by thousands of careful observations.

CHAPTER VIII

ANALYZING THE MAN
NINE FUNDAMENTAL PHYSICAL VARIABLES

IF THERE were an absolutely reliable method of interpreting human character by the lines on the palms of a man's hands, or the bumps under the hair of his head, it would be of comparatively little value in the ordinary interests and activities of life. If by elaborate tests, with special instruments, one could learn all about the aptitudes and character of a willing subject, the method would be almost as valueless for practical use. We meet and deal with people under conditions which would make it impossible either to examine the palms of their hands or the bumps on their heads or to subject them to psychological tests. The most important relationships with other people oftentimes occur when one must observe them at a distance, and perhaps for but a few moments, when they are wearing hats and gloves, when perhaps the light may be poor, and under other conditions which will enable one to make only the most general observations. It therefore becomes necessary in analyzing the man to enumerate and classify the most easily observable of his physical characteristics, which give a key to his physical, mental, and psychical aptitudes and character.

VARIABLES DEFINED

All normal men are alike in most of their physical characteristics. They have the same number of bones and muscles, parts and organs; the same number and general arrangement of features. They differ from one another in other ways. One man is light; another is dark. One man is tall; another is short. One man is sharp-featured; another is broad-, flat-faced. One man is coarse, heavy, and crude; another delicate and refined. Colour, size, form, and texture are some of the physical attributes in which men differ or vary from one another. We may therefore call these attributes *variables*. It is in these physical variables and the variations in character which accompany them that we find a scientific basis for analyzing the man.

In the study of these variables, research and investigation are undertaken to find answers to such questions as these, for example: Why do men vary in colour? What are the hereditary and environmental causes of their variation? Would these same causes and others associated with them produce any variation in other physical attributes, and in mental and psychical characteristics? What would these variations be? In studying men of different colour, do we actually find such variations in character? In the same way, analysis is made of the causes of other variations, and the effects of these causes upon character.

After a great deal of study and experimentation we finally determined upon nine physical variables as fundamentals, and as affording ample data for the analysis of human character in employment work. These are: (1) Colour, (2) Form, (3) Size, (4) Structure, (5) Texture, (6) Consistency, (7) Proportion, (8) Expression, (9) Condition.

It is not only impossible to present completely and in detail in a work of this nature the entire science of character analysis by the observational method, but instruction in this science is not the function of the present volume. A brief consideration of underlying principles, methods of application, and the usefulness of the science in employment work will, however, not be amiss. We shall therefore treat each of these nine fundamental variables, showing our method of approach and, in a brief outline, what their variations in the individual reveal. In our discussion of colour and form we enter at some length into the evolutionary causes of both physical and psychical variations. The other variables are treated more briefly.

COLOUR

In the paintings and pottery of ancient Egypt, Greece, Rome, and Spain, divinity, royalty, nobility, and aristocracy are represented by white skin, blue eyes, and flaxen hair. Until very recently, most dolls had blue eyes and yellow hair, even in countries where their little mothers were as brown as berries. There are other interesting and significant evidences of an age-old feeling, amounting almost to instinct, that there are differences in character between blonds and brunettes as marked as their differences in colour. There is no variable among human beings so striking as that of colour, none so easily observable, and none which has made so strong an appeal to scientific investigators as well as to popular imagination.

An inquiry into the biological causes of variations in human colour, into the mental and psychical causes accompanying these, and into the historical and prehistorical causes of the attitude toward blonds revealed in art, in literature, in the drama, and in popular speech, will aid us in understanding the many differences between blonds and brunettes.

PIGMENTATION

The immediate cause of the differences in colour among human beings is the relative amount of pigmentation in hair, skin, iris, and retina. Scientists have long been at work striving to discover the cause of pigmentation, and especially the cause for variation in the amount of pigmentation. In general, it is well known that dark or heavily pigmented races inhabit the tropics, and that lighter or less pigmented races inhabit the temperate and north temperate zones.

For a long time scientists have worked upon a theory that heavy pigmentation, resulting in dark colour, helped the inhabitants of hot countries to keep cool. This was because of the known fact that dark bodies radiate heat more rapidly than light bodies. Of two pieces of iron of the same size and shape, one black and the other painted white, and both heated to the same temperature, the black one will cool off much more quickly than the white one. This is in accordance with the law of radiation. A difficulty was met, however, when the law of absorption was taken into consideration. According to this law, dark bodies absorb heat from sources of higher temperature than themselves much more readily than light ones. If a black iron and a white iron are both placed upon the same stove, the black one will heat up much more quickly than the white one. It is probable that both of these laws have some effect in determining the evolution of colour. It is well known that black people in the tropics keep in the shade as much as possible, and are very largely nocturnal in their habits. Comparatively few are seen abroad or at work during the hours just before, or just after, noon. Keeping in the darkness and shade, they make the most of their natural ability to radiate heat. By avoiding as far as possible exposing themselves to the direct rays of the sun, they absorb heat as little as possible. On the other hand, the lighter coloured races in the cold North could not absorb much even if they were black, and their slower rate of radiation enables them to conserve better the natural heat of their bodies.

Negroes find great difficulty in keeping warm in cold climates. They require more clothing in cold weather than whites; prefer to keep indoors, and keep their quarters so hot that they seem stifling to white people. But the theory that the laws of radiation and absorption explain everything about pigmentation, and that man's colour has been evolved wholly for the purpose of enabling him to adapt himself to the degree of temperature of his environment, does not satisfy. The Eskimo, living in the cold Arctic regions, has black hair, gray or brown eyes, and a yellow or brown skin. Dwellers on the cold northern plains of Asia and North America are brown and yellow, while certain tribes in the heavily forested but hot, moist mountains of northern Africa are blond. These considerations have led to a further study of the cause of pigmentation.

SUNLIGHT THE CAUSE OF PIGMENTATION

In 1895, Josef Von Schmaedel read a paper before the Anthropological Society of Munich, announcing the theory that pigmentation in man was evolved for the purpose of excluding actinic or short rays of light which destroy living protoplasm. This set Major (now Lieutenant-Colonel, retired) Charles E. Woodruff, A. M., M. D., Surgeon U. S. Army, upon a systematic search for data to prove or disprove Von Schmaedel's theory. In 1905, Major Woodruff published his book, "The Effects of Tropical Light on White Men."* In this fascinating work, Major Woodruff champions the theory of Von Schmaedel and gives a great mass of data, gathered from many scientists, as well as the result of his own original research — all favourable to the correctness of the theory that the shorter violet and ultraviolet, actinic rays of light first stimulate, then exhaust, and finally destroy living protoplasm, and that pigmentation in both men and animals has been evolved for the purpose of excluding these actinic rays of sunlight from the tissues of the body. Sunburn, sunstroke, and the

*Rebman Co., New York.

dangerous burns of the X-ray, radium, and other sources of short rays, as well as the popularly known fact that sunlight kills bacteria, are all evidences of the destructive effect of actinic rays.

Another evidence of the relationship between pigmentation and sunlight, rather than sun's heat, is the fact that albinos — who are unpigmented — are excessively sensitive to light, while not any more sensitive to heat than others of the same race. According to this theory, also, the brunetteness of the Eskimo, the North American Indian, and the dweller in the northern part of Asia is explained. The Eskimo requires his pigmentation as a protection against the blinding glare of snow and ice. The plains of northern Asia and North America, while cold, are also largely free from fog and cloud, so that considerable pigmentation is needed in these parts of the world as a protection against light. According to Dr. Carl Beck, blonds are far more liable to burns and lesions by X-rays than brunettes, the extreme brunette being almost immune.*

BLOND AND BRUNETTE RACES

Still further confirmation of this theory is found in the evolution of extreme blondness in northwestern Europe, on the plains, and among the heavily forested mountains in the neighbourhood

*New York Medical Record, January 13, 1900.

of the Baltic Sea. This is the cloudiest, foggiest, darkest region on the face of the earth, and is the cradle of the Scandinavian and Teutonic races, both of which are predominantly blond. Anthropologists violently differ as to the place where the blond or white races were evolved. Most of them, however, agree that primitive man was brunette and that blondness has been evolved as the result of either forced or voluntary migration of the primitive brunette to cold, dark, cloudy northwestern Europe. The climate of this part of Europe is rigorous and severe.

At this point let us define our use of the terms blond and brunette. In popular usage a blond is a person of the white race with extremely light hair, blue eyes, and pink-and-white skin; a brunette a person of the white race with dark hair, brown eyes, and sallow or very light olive skin. As we use the terms here, all races of mankind are divided into two classes — those with white skins and those with dark skins. The albino is the most extreme blond; the black negro the most extreme brunette. Those fairer than halfway between the two are blond; those darker, brunette. According to this classification, most of those ordinarily called brunettes are blonds. They belong to "white" races. They manifest the characteristics of blonds in inverse proportion to their degree of pigmentation.

EVOLUTION OF BLOND RACES

The necessities of life in the harsh environment where blondness was evolved are more numerous and at the same time more difficult to obtain than in a milder one. Man requires more food, more shelter, more clothing, more fuel, than in a warm climate. Whereas fruits, vegetables, fish, flesh, and fowl are comparatively easy to secure in warm latitudes, they are scarce, difficult to secure, and require much more preparation in the higher latitudes. Under Northern climatic conditions, then, only the largest, strongest, healthiest, most intelligent, most hopeful, most courageous, and most aggressive individuals would survive. The natural result would be the evolution of a race of men and women endowed with robust physical, mental, and psychical characteristics. Since the relatively abundant pigmentation of the primitive first settler in these dark countries was not needed as a protection against light, blondness was gradually evolved along with the characteristics just mentioned.

A process of evolution, therefore, having produced a vigorous, aggressive blond race, conquerors of a harsh and severe environment, these qualities of the race sent them southward, eastward, and westward to become the conquerors and rulers of brunette races less aggressive, less bold, less domineering, less vigorous, because their more kindly environment had not necessitated the evolution of these rugged traits. Prehistoric evidence in abundance indicates that a conquering race of tall, vigorous, fair-haired, blue-eyed, white-skinned men migrated in successive waves over Europe, Asia Minor, northern Africa, Persia, India, Ceylon, Java, and perhaps as far east as the Philippine Islands. This race of men called themselves Aryans, and wherever they went forced their language upon the conquered brunette races. How long ago these prehistoric migrations of Aryans began is lost in antiquity, but there are evidences in the Pyramids of intruding white men as early as three or four thousand years before Christ. It is known that there was an invasion of white men into Greece 2000 to 1000 B. C. However early this migration may have been, it was so long ago that ancient Sanskrit, formerly spoken and written in India and Persia, classic Greek and Latin, as well as ancient and modern German, French, Spanish, Italian, Dutch, Danish, Swedish, Norwegian, English, Gaelic, and Welsh languages, and many dialects now spoken in India, all bear unmistakable evidence of their common origin in the Aryan tongue.

It is significant that Hellenes, the name by which the ancient Greeks called themselves; Celts and

Gaels, names given to themselves by the ancient inhabitants of Great Britain and Ireland; and Aryans, the general name given to themselves by the conquering races to which we have referred, all mean "white men." Some high anthropological authorities do not accept the theory of the Aryan race. Some assign the place of its origin to Asia instead of Europe. But the majority favour the outline we have given — and the preponderance of evidence seems to be with them.

CHARACTERISTICS OF EARLY BLOND RACES

These early white men were tall, vigorous, restless, courageous, aggressive, and brainy, but they lacked culture. They excelled in warfare, in navigation, in exploration, but they are always called crude, barbarian, rough, and brutal by ancient writers. Having conquered the brunette natives of the various countries to which they migrated, the white men proved themselves to be wonderful organizers, creators, builders, rulers, and captains of industry. They early adopted the culture, arts, and letters developed through long centuries of patient plodding by the brunette peoples, among whom they intruded and over whom they ruled. They built up wonderful civilizations, great cities, and wealthy and powerful nations. The ruins of these Aryan creations are scattered through

ANALYZING THE MAN

Java, Ceylon, India, Persia, Syria, Egypt, Greece, Macedonia, Italy, and Spain.

We therefore have the picture of civilization running back from eight to ten thousand years, with the ruling classes, the nobility, the aristocracy always blond, and the peasantry, the working classes, the subordinates in the scheme of things, always brunette. This fact is reflected in the Aryan languages, in the ancient paintings and statuary referred to at the beginning of this chapter, and in the almost instinctive glorification of the blond in art, in literature, on the stage, and in the vernacular. All occidental civilization, and a great deal of oriental civilization, has been built up and ruled from the very earliest times by white men. In many ancient governments the king or emperor was deified, and so gods and goddesses and all supernatural beings are represented as blonds.

It is interesting to note in this connection that the inhabitants of modern Java, Ceylon, India, Persia, Syria, Asia Minor, Greece, Turkey, Italy, Spain, and France are now predominantly brunette. Many anthropologists agree that the blond Aryans who built up these old civilizations and left their language as a legacy have entirely died out. The reason for this disappearance of the tall, vigorous, restless blond is not so well understood. It ought to be clear to the thoughtful observer, however, that if blondness was evolved in cold, dark, northwestern Europe, then the extreme white Aryan race was out of its natural environment in these lands where there is an excess of light, against which they had little pigmentation as a protection. It is a well-known fact that there is no third generation of white men in India. Woodruff presents an abundance of evidence to prove that the effect of an excess of sunlight, with its destructive actinic rays, is first to stimulate, then exhaust and degenerate, and finally to extirpate the white races. He assigns the degeneracy and fall of all ancient civilizations in hot countries to the effects of tropical and subtropical sunlight upon their blond rulers.

TWO FACTS ABOUT BLONDS

Statistics show that blonds are becoming relatively less numerous than brunettes in England, the United States, New Zealand, Australia, and South Africa, notwithstanding the constant fresh migrations of blonds to these countries from northwestern Europe. Statistics also show many forms of physical, nervous, and mental degeneracy of blonds in tropical regions, of the second or third generations of blonds in subtropical climates, and of later generations of blonds in those parts of the temperate and north temperate zones where there is an abundance of sunlight. All of these facts are of great scientific value to the student of variations in physique, in appearance, and in character among human beings.

Two fundamental facts about blonds stand out from all this mass of evidence and are the key by which we may best understand their physical, mental, and psychical qualities: (1) Blondness was evolved in an environment which permitted the survival of those only who were most vigorous, most intelligent, most aggressive, most creative, most active, and most capable of adapting themselves to extremes of heat and cold, feast and famine, altitude, and occupation. (2) In countries where there is a great deal of light, blonds are suffering more or less from too much stimulation of brain and nerves, and oftentimes from brain and nerve exhaustion, and consequent physical, mental, and psychical degeneracy.

EVOLUTION OF THE BRUNETTE

In studying the brunette we shall understand better his characteristics if we remember that his brunetteness was evolved, in the great majority of cases, in a warm, pleasant climate where his necessities were comparatively few. Man requires less food, less clothing, less shelter, less fuel in a warm climate than in a cold one. In addition to requiring less of all these things, the brunette found them all easy to obtain from the abundance of animal and vegetable life around him. His surroundings were comfortable, conducive to quiet and physical inactivity. Since there was plenty to supply his few wants close at hand, he did not need to take to sea or travel far by land. Receiving most of his necessary warmth from outside sources, he did not need as much oxygen as the blond, who had to breathe in great quantities of it that he might sustain internal oxygenization and thus produce heat for himself. As a result of the same conditions, all processes of metabolism and katabolism in the brunette were slower than these processes in the blond. Whereas the blond was required to expend all of his mental and physical energy in active, aggressive combat with his harsh environment in order to obtain the material means of life, the brunette, in a kindlier environment and in the midst of plenty, had both energy and time to spare.

With these scientific facts as to the evolution of blondness and brunetteness in mind, a thoughtful, logical person should be able to determine accurately the physical, mental, and psychical differences between blonds and brunettes.

CHARACTERISTICS OF BLONDS

The keynote of the physical characteristics of the *normal blond* is positiveness. He inclines to be tall, robust, with a superabundance of buoyant, radiant health and vigour. Since his race was evolved in a cold, dark, harsh environment, all of his physical processes are rapid and active. In order to maintain heat, it was necessary for his ancestors to eat and digest large quantities of food and breathe in a great deal of oxygen. To maintain health and survive in their environment, they needed strong, reliable circulations and circulatory systems. With digestion, respiration, and circulation positive and active, processes of elimination needed to be similarly quick and active. All of these characteristics, as well as the low temperature in which they lived, necessitated great muscular activity; as did also their need for food and clothing.

Because of his heredity and racial environment, therefore, the normal blond is characterized in every department of his physical being by positiveness, rapidity, adaptability, energy, and activity. It is for these reasons that a blond seldom suffers from chronic diseases. He becomes ill quickly and dies or recovers quickly.

Since quickness and aggressiveness are physical attributes of the blond; since in his hunting, his sailing, and his fighting he has always been called upon for quick explosions of tremendous energy followed by periods of recuperation, the blond is not particularly well fitted for long-sustained physical action. He expends his abundant energy too rapidly. In athletics, therefore, blonds excel in the sprints and dashes, in jumping, throwing, vaulting, and other such contests; while the brunettes are better adapted to long runs, wrestling, prize fighting, and other contests where endurance is the prime requisite.

The early environment of the blond races was damp and rainy, and their mode of life required both swimming and wading. Blonds are therefore, as a rule, fond of water. The majority of great swimmers, skaters, oarsmen, and yachtsmen are blonds. The early Aryans were the first navigators. During the time of the Aryan civilization in Phœnicia, the Phœnicians were the great maritime nation; and it was when the Aryans ruled in Persia, in Greece, in Rome, in Carthage, in Spain, and in France, that these different nations maintained supremacy of sea power. It was when the Aryan rulers had been eliminated by excessive sunlight that their sea power waned.

The mental characteristics of blonds are the results partly of the influence of their heredity and environment directly upon their mental nature, and partly arise from their physical condition. Since the brain of the blond was evolved in an

ANALYZING THE MAN

environment requiring the constant exercise of intelligence, he is naturally creative, resourceful, inventive, original. These qualities, it will readily be seen, fit in perfectly with those which are the result of his exuberant health.

THE DOMINEERING BLOND

The man who has a good digestion, a good circulation, who breathes deeply, and whose general health is robust and positive, will naturally be optimistic, hopeful, exuberant, eager, and fearless. Such a man is willing to take a chance, speculative, impatient, restless, always sighing for new worlds to conquer. The early struggle for existence of the blond races led them far afield. They hunted over miles of territory. They hunted in the mountains and on the plains. They went to sea in ships. Their very climate was freakish and changeable. As a result of these environmental influences, the blond developed an eager and active disposition, and is fond of change, loves variety, is happiest when he has many irons in the fire, and easily turns his attention from one interest to another. Because of these qualities, and because of the joy of conquest developed through ages of triumph over unfriendly environment, the blond loves to rule. He is inclined to be domineering. He loves to handle and manage large affairs and come in contact with life at as many points as possible. Because of his exuberant health, his splendid circulation, and his naturally optimistic, hopeful, courageous disposition, the blond likes excitement, crowds, gayety. He is a good mixer — makes acquaintances readily with all kinds of people, but, on account of his changeable nature, is liable to be fickle. Thus everywhere blonds push into the limelight, engage in politics, promoting and building up great enterprises, selling, advertising, organizing, colonizing, creating, and inventing. It is for this reason that blonds predominate among royalty, nobility, and aristocracy. This has been observed by many investigators. In the *Monthly Review* for August, 1901, page 93, Havelock Ellis says:

HAVELOCK ELLIS ON BLONDS AND BRUNETTES

"It is clear that a high index of pigmentation, or an excess of fairness, prevails among the men of restless and ambitious temperament, the sanguine, energetic men, the men who easily dominate their fellows and who get on in life, the men who recruit the aristocracy and who doubtless largely form the plutocracy. It is significant that the group of low-class men — artisans and peasants — and the men of religion, whose mission in life it is to preach resignation to a higher will, are both notably of dark complexion. While the men of action thus

ANALYZING THE MAN

tend to be fair, men of thought, it seems to me, show some tendency to be dark."

On pages 95 and 96 he says: "It so happens that an interesting and acute psychological study of the fair and dark populations of Norway has lately been made by Dr. A. M. Hansen. This investigation has revealed differences even more marked between the fair and dark than may easily be discovered in our own islands, and this is not surprising, since our racial elements have been more thoroughly mixed. The fair population, he tells us, is made up of the born aristocrats, active, outspoken, progressive, with a passion for freedom and independence, caring nothing for equality; the dark population is reserved and suspicious, very conservative, lacking in initiative, caring little for freedom, but with a passion for equality. The fair people are warlike, quarrelsome when drunk, and furnish, in proportion to numbers, three times as many men for the volunteer forces as the dark people; the latter, though brave sailors, abhor war, and are very religious, subscribing to foreign missions nearly three times as much per head as is furnished by fair people, who are inclined to be irreligious. The fair people value money and all that money can buy, while the dark people are indifferent to money. The reality of mental distinction is shown by the fact that a map of the proportion of conservative voters in elections to the Storthing exactly corresponds to an anthropological map of the country, the conservative majority being found in the dark and broad-headed districts. While, however, the fair population is the most irreligious and progressive, the dark population is by no means behind in the production of intellect, and the region it inhabits has produced many eminent men."

In the same article, on page 97, he says: "It may also be remarked that the characteristics of the fair population are especially masculine qualities; while the characteristics of the dark population are more peculiarly feminine qualities. It so happens also that women, as is now beginning to be generally recognized by anthropologists, tend to be somewhat darker than men."

WOODRUFF ON BLONDS AND BRUNETTES

On page 142, "The Effects of Tropical Light on White Men," Major Woodruff says: "The fair man tends to be bold, energetic, restless, and domineering, not because he is fair, but because he belongs to an aboriginal fair stock of people who possess those qualities; while the dark man tends to be resigned and religious and imitative, yet highly intelligent, not because he is dark, but because he belongs to a dark stock possessing these

Fig. 1. American Indian. Observe high nose and strong chin

characteristics. While, however, the fair population is the most irreligious and progressive, the dark population is by no means behind in the production of intellect."

One of the first thoughts of the average reader of this chapter will be of some blond or brunette who contradicts every one of these generalizations. Lest this be discouraging, we call attention to several important considerations: First, there are many blonds and brunettes, who, for pathological reasons, are not normal; second, albinos or near albinos are not the only blonds; third, the observation of an unpracticed eye is not always reliable; fourth, there are eight other variables yet to be observed, each with its many variations and their important significance; fifth, the characteristics accompanying variations in colour find many avenues of expression, not all of them patent to the casual observer.

CHARACTERISTICS OF BRUNETTES

Just as the normal blond is physically and mentally consistent with what might be expected of one of his evolution and history, so is the normal brunette. Since the brunette races were evolved in a kindlier climate than the blond, less physical and mental positiveness was required of them, and they have been able to survive without the exuberant health, vigour, intelligence, resourcefulness, and aggressiveness required of blonds. Their respiration, digestion, circulation, and elimination are all slower and more moderate than in the blond. Since size has not been necessary for their survival, they do not incline to be so large as blonds; nor are they so active, so quick, or in any way physically so positive. Brunettes require less food and breathe less oxygen than blonds. Since all physical processes of brunettes are slower, they expend their energy less rapidly, and are therefore more enduring. They do not become ill so quickly, but are more subject to chronic diseases.

Because his environment has not required it, and because of his negative physical nature, the brunette is not so bold, not so aggressive, not so recklessly indifferent to consequences as the blond. For these reasons, and because his mode of life as well as his climate has tended to sameness, the brunette is more conservative, more constant. In keeping with all of these qualities, the brunette does not seek the limelight, crowds, dominating position, and excitement, but prefers a few friends, well beloved, a quiet home, the affection of his family and pets, and an opportunity to enjoy the beauties of nature. Because the brunette has not been compelled to give all of his time and energy to a struggle for his life with harsh material condi-

Fig. 2. A Turkish Parade. Turks, evolved in cold, light northern Asia, are brunettes with convex noses

ANALYZING THE MAN

tions, he has evolved a tendency to introspection, to the development of philosophy, religion, mysteries, and other products of metaphysical and spiritual activities. It is significant that Christianity, Buddhism, Confucianism, and Mohammedanism — the four principal religions of the world — have their origin and their most devoted adherents among brunette peoples.

ORIENT AND OCCIDENT

The difference between the Orient and the Occident is very largely a difference between blonds and brunettes. It is typical of the oriental brunette that he should incline to mysticism, occultism, psychism, meditation, self-denial, and non-resistance, living on a meagre diet and rather indifferent to material things. It is also characteristic of the occidental blond that he should be materialistic, commercial, scientific, manufacturing, an organizer of trusts and combinations, a builder of railroads and empires, interested chiefly in the things he can see, hear, smell, taste, and feel, and giving the unseen world but secondary consideration.

The brunette, having time at his disposal, has evolved patience, and with it a disposition for detail, for minute specialization. Not having a genius for organization and government, he is usually willing to permit the domineering blond to take this burden off his hands. To-day, wherever there is stable government, it is either in the hands or under the influence of blonds — white men. India is ruled by blond England, as is Egypt. Turkey and the Balkan States have been in a state of suppressed and active turbulence ever since the line of blond rulers died out, and are now being reduced to something like order by blond Europe. Mexico and some of the South and Central American republics achieved whatever measure of stability they had under the rule of blond Goths and descendants of Goths from Spain. Now that these white strains have been killed off by excessive sunlight these countries have become so unstable that some kind of white protectorate seems necessary.

Prison statistics show that the blond is most frequently guilty of crimes of passion and impulse, crimes arising from his gambling propensities and ill-considered promotion schemes; while the brunette is more likely to commit crimes of deliberation, specialization, detail, such as murder, counterfeiting, forgeries, conspiracy, etc. Because the blond is healthy, optimistic, and naturally good-humoured, he eliminates anger, hatred, melancholy, discouragement, and all other negative feelings from his mind as easily as he eliminates waste products from his body. Because he is naturally

Fig. 3. A Group of Negro Boys. Note primitive forehead of boy in middle of rear line. Also flat noses and convex mouths and chins

ANALYZING THE MAN

slow, cautious, conservative, and inclined to be serious and thoughtful, the brunette is far more liable to harbour resentment, to cherish a grudge, to plan revenge, to see the dark side of life, and often to be melancholy and pessimistic.

The same qualities that cause the blond to be cheerful and optimistic when things go wrong, give him a tendency to permit things, if they seem trivial to him, to go wrong. On the other hand, the same qualities that cause the brunette to be careful and painstaking with minute details also incline him to worry and grow despondent when trouble comes.

INDICATIONS OF COLOUR SUMMED UP

In brief, always and everywhere, the normal blond has positive, dynamic, driving, aggressive, domineering, impatient, active, quick, hopeful, speculative, changeable, and variety-loving characteristics; while the normal brunette has negative, static, conservative, imitative, submissive, cautious, painstaking, patient, plodding, slow, deliberate, serious, thoughtful, specializing characteristics.

In applying this law of colour to people of the white race, the method is simple. The less the pigmentation in any individual, the more marked will be the characteristics of the blond in his physical, mental, and psychical nature; the greater the degree of pigmentation, the more marked the characteristics of the brunette.

FORM
The Evolution of Form

Primitive man was not only brunette, according to anthropologists, but had a short, wide, low-bridged nose, with large, round nostrils leading almost directly to the throat. Primitive man doubtless inhabited the tropical and subtropical regions of the earth. Dwelling in a warm climate, he was slow in all his muscular and organic reactions, had comparatively little need to develop bodily heat, and was not compelled to great activity in order to obtain his relatively meagre necessities of life. For all of these reasons, therefore, primitive man required only moderate supplies of oxygen. His breathing was therefore shallow and slow. The warm, moist air of his natural environment needed little or no tempering before entering his lungs. Therefore a short, wide air-passage fitted his requirements admirably. It was all the better because the air of the tropics is rarefied by heat and contains less oxygen in a given volume than cold air.

When man, either voluntarily or as the result of overcrowding, migrated into colder and harsher climates, conditions were changed. The air, being

Fig. 4. Filipino Girls. They have the characteristic concave foreheads and noses, and convex mouths and chins of brunette races

Copyright by Underwood & Underwood, N. Y.

cold, was more condensed, and contained more oxygen in proportion to its volume than air in the warmer climates. Short, wide air-passages to the lungs were not necessary. On the other hand, they were a disadvantage, as cold air quickly killed off those with the flattest, widest noses and shallowest lungs — just as it kills negroes by pneumonia, bronchitis, and tuberculosis in our Northern climes to-day. While the greater density of the air increased its richness in oxygen in proportion to volume, its lower temperature necessitated a larger consumption of oxygen in order to maintain bodily heat. There was also an increased demand for oxygen due to the greater muscular activity needed to hunt down, capture, carry, and otherwise provide food, clothing, shelter, and fuel. So man in his rigorous environment breathed greater volumes of air, and at the same time required the air he breathed to be warmed and moistened before reaching his lungs.

EVOLUTION OF THE LARGE, HIGH NOSE

Since those with the shortest and flattest noses were killed off by the climate, it follows that those with the longest, highest, narrowest noses survived. This process of selection developed a race with noses high in the bridge, well set out from the face, and with narrow, elongated nostrils. Cold air, though admitted through such a nose in large quantities, would be drawn in thin ribbons over and around moistened and heated surfaces, and thus prepared for the lungs. The high, thin nose was therefore evolved in the same environment with blondness and is associated, along with blondness, with nobility and aristocracy by artists, poets, dramatists, and the people generally in both ancient and modern times. Next to colour, therefore, the nose as seen in profile is perhaps one of the most ancient as well as one of the most easily observed and popularly regarded indications of character.

Not all high, thin noses, however, were evolved along with blondness. The brown and yellow races of the cold, light northern plains of Asia and America also have them. Such noses are shown in figures 1 and 2 (American Indians and Turks). The faces of brunette peoples who live in warm, moist climates show how common is the broad, flat nose among them. See figures 3 and 4 (Negroes and Filipinos.)

The height and thinness of the nose among the people of India has been found to correspond very closely with their height of caste. H. H. Risley in his book, "The Types and Castes of Bengal," pages 80-81, says: "If we take a series of castes in Bengal, Behar, or the Northwest Province and arrange them in the order of the average nasal

Fig. 5. Chinese on Man of War. Note predominance of concave foreheads and noses, convex mouths and chins

Photograph by Underwood & Underwood.

index, so that the caste with the finest nose shall be at the top, and that with the coarsest at the bottom of the list, it will be found that this order substantially corresponds with the accepted order of social precedence. The casteless tribes — Kols, Korwas, Munda, and the like — who have not yet entered the Brahmanical system, occupy the lowest place. Then come the vermin-eating Muskars and the leather-dressing Chamars. . . . From them we pass to the trading Khatris, the landholding Babhan, and the upper crust of Hindu society. It is scarcely a paradox to lay down as a law for the caste organization of eastern India that a man's social status varies in inverse ratio to the width of his nose. . . . The remarkable correspondence between the gradations of type as brought out by certain indices, and the gradations of social precedence, enables us to conclude that community of race, and not, as has frequently been argued, community of function, is the real determining principle of the caste system. Everywhere we find high social position associated with a certain physical type and, conversely, low social position with a markedly different type." Bengal is a presidency in northern India, much of it being of high altitude, where cold and dryness have had their effect upon the nose as well as upon the character of the people.

From our own records we find that out of 997 white people examined in all parts of America, 851, or 85.28 per cent., had high noses, and 146, or 14.72 per cent., low noses.

The significant point in regard to the contour or *form* of the nose as seen in profile is this: The high, prominent nose enables its possessor to breathe in large quantities of oxygen in cold air. It was evolved in the midst of environments necessitating great *activity* and *aggressiveness*. It is therefore always associated with *positive energy*. The low, short, "sway-back," or flat nose is best adapted to breathe warm, moist, rarefied air. It was evolved in the midst of an environment not requiring much activity. It is therefore associated with comparative inactivity and moderate or deficient energy.

EVOLUTION OF THE HIGH, SLOPING FOREHEAD

An examination of figures 3, 4, and 5 reveals some interesting and significant facts about foreheads. Among the most primitive and most backward races and individuals we find the forehead low, short, narrow, and receding — small in every dimension. Among most civilized and semi-civilized brunette peoples the forehead is much higher, much wider, and inclined to be more prominent at or just below the hair-line than at the brows, as in Chinese, Japanese, and Malays. (See figures

Fig. 6. A splendid example of convex upper, concave lower, profile

ANALYZING THE MAN

4 and 5.) Among white people the forehead is high and wide. In some individuals it is more prominent at the hair-line than at the brows, but in the majority much more prominent at the brows than above. (See figures 6, 7, 8, and 9.) Our observations, taken upon 1,994 whites, show that 1,701, or 85.27 per cent., have foreheads prominent at the brows and receding above; 293, or 14.73 per cent., prominent above and flat at the brows.

The contour, or *form*, of the forehead *as seen in profile* is more or less closely associated with colour, and presents considerations worthy of careful study and comparison. Popular opinion relates the size and shape of the forehead with the degree and type of intellectual power. People call a man who is interested in abstruse, intellectual matters a high-brow, and the man who is grossly material in his thought a low-brow. Anthropologists and physiological psychologists add their testimony by agreeing, almost unanimously, that the higher intellectual functions of the brain are performed by the frontal section of the cerebrum.

Whether there is any real causal connection between the size and form of the forehead and the degree and kind of intellectual power possessed by the individual is a question, the discussion of which we shall leave to others. We call attention, however, once more to the illustrations. Figures 4 and

5 show that civilized and semi-civilized dark races generally have foreheads prominent above and comparatively flat at the brows. As we have seen, the brunette inclines to be thoughtful, meditative, introspective, philosophic, and theoretical, rather than practical intellectually; while the blond inclines to be imaginative, inventive, material, commercial, scientific, and practical.

Since the brunette was interested chiefly in dreams, fancies, philosophies, creeds, poems, and in the world of spirit and thought in general, he developed the power of abstract reasoning, analysis, correlation, and the perception of intellectual and spiritual values, leaving his powers of perception of material and tangible things comparatively undeveloped. Since the blond was interested chiefly in material things, he trained and developed keen and reliable sense perceptions, and the ability to see things in their practical relationships. Therefore the "bulging" forehead is the forehead of meditation, of dreams and fancies, of abstract reasoning, of philosophies and creeds, and oftentimes of those delicate perceptions of the incongruity of ideas which we call a sense of humour. The high, sloping forehead is associated with a keen, practical, matter-of-fact intellect. Such an intellect gains its knowledge readily and quickly through the senses. It demands facts, but is com-

Fig. 7. Savonarola. Extreme convex form of profile. Note especially convex mouth

ANALYZING THE MAN

paratively uninterested in the reasons for the facts. This type of intellect forms its conclusions quickly upon presentation of facts, especially of facts in concrete form, without taking the time to reason deeply or ponder over them. In general, then, the form of forehead which slopes back from the brows (see figure 6) is found with a quick, energetic, positive intellect; that which is prominent above (see figure 5) is found with a slow, meditative intellect of moderate or deficient energy.

EVOLUTION OF FORM OF MOUTH AND CHIN

That we may study the face as a whole, let us also observe the contour of the mouth and chin as seen in profile. The dweller in the kindly, gentle climes of the tropics and subtropics finds most of his food in the form of ripe fruit. This is not only soft and easy of mastication but also so easy of digestion as to be in some cases almost predigested. The dweller in the cold, dark regions of the North is required to cut and tear and grind his food with his teeth. Such fruits as grow in his clime are harder and tougher than those found in the tropics. He also eats a great deal of grain, which has to be ground, and in ancient days was mostly ground by his own teeth. Nuts had to be cracked, and were frequently cracked by the teeth. Fish, flesh, and fowl were cut and torn and crushed by the teeth. Eskimo women prepare and soften leather by gnawing off the fat and gristle and chewing the skins. In this way the primitive dweller in the North developed a wide, deep jaw and chin, which not only afforded an adequate setting for his large teeth but a firm fastening for the muscles of mastication. (See figures 6, 10, and 16.)

Civilized and semi-civilized dark races as shown in figures 3, 4, and 5 incline either to narrow, receding chins or short, wide, receding chins. Is it strange that "strong" chins in literature and in the popular mind should be associated with courage, will-power, defiance, endurance, and persistence, and that "weak" or receding chins are held to be indications of a degree of deficiency in these qualities? The wide, deep chin, prominent at the lower point, as seen in profile, was evolved in the midst of an environment requiring courage, determination, and endurance. The short, narrow, receding chin was evolved in the midst of an environment requiring relatively little of these qualities.

It is only natural that in the narrow, contracted, under-developed jaw and chin the teeth are crowded and pushed forward. This gives the mouth, as seen in profile, a protruding or prominent form. In the broad, square jaw, the teeth, having plenty of room, arrange themselves in a broader, flatter curve and stand either vertically in the jaws or

Fig. 8. Kaiser Wilhelm II. Good example of pure convex form of profile. Note great energy indicated by nose

pointed slightly inward rather than outward. This arrangement and position of the teeth gives the entire mouth, as seen in profile, a flatter, less prominent, and even receding aspect. Figures 3, 4, 5, and 7 show the prominent mouth and teeth; figures 6, 10, the flat or receding mouth and teeth.

DIGESTION AND CHARACTER

The articulation of protruding teeth is often poor. It is not easy for them to masticate food. Easily digested food is, as we have seen, the principal part of the diet where this form of mouth is evolved. The tendency, therefore, is toward quick, rather weak, digestion. And an unreliable digestion leads to irritability, cynicism, scolding, and "grouchiness." A less prominent and protruding arrangement of the teeth gives them more room for development. It also affords better articulation and makes better mastication possible. This arrangement of teeth having been evolved in regions where most of the food obtainable required time and vigour to digest, the tendency of evolution was therefore toward a slow, strong, reliable digestion. Such a digestion is conducive to abundant nourishment — and the mild, sweet, good-natured, cheerful disposition which naturally results from a sound digestion and sufficient food. A hungry animal — or a hungry man — is often cross and impatient.

And one whose digestion is poor is in a constant state of partial starvation. A prominent mouth, therefore, was evolved along with a quick, unreliable digestion — a receding mouth with a slow, reliable digestion. Hence a prominent mouth is associated with irritability and impatience — a receding mouth with mildness and sweetness.

We have now considered briefly the evolution of form of forehead, nose, mouth, and chin, as seen in profile. We have also considered very briefly the significance of form in each case. Note carefully the following facts: First, form always relates to the contour of a feature *as seen in profile*. Second, in considering form we always give attention to whether the feature is prominent and protruding, or somewhat concave and receding. With these points clearly in mind, let us now construct a human face, as seen in profile, with forehead prominent at the brows and receding above, with the eyes large and prominent, with the nose high in the bridge, long, and standing well out from the face, with teeth and mouth protruding and prominent, and with chin short and receding. Such a face is well represented by figures 7, 8, and 9.

Now let us construct another face, with forehead prominent above and flat at the brows, eyes deep-set and small, nose short, sway-back, or snubbed, teeth and mouth receding, and chin long, broad,

Fig. 9. An American Engineer. Pure convex form of profile. Note especially prominent brows

ANALYZING THE MAN

and prominent at the lower point. Such a face is well represented in figure 10.

Now let us construct still another face, with a straight forehead, about equally prominent above and at the brows, with eyes neither deep-set nor protruding, with a straight, medium-sized nose, with a mouth neither prominent nor receding, and a chin whose form, as seen in profile, is in a straight line with the forehead, eyes, nose, and mouth. Such a face is well represented in figure 11.

THREE PRIMARY FORMS OF FACE

Now let us examine carefully these three faces. The face shown in figure 9 is convex in form, as seen in profile. The face in figure 10 is concave in form, as seen in profile. The face in figure 11 is plane, as seen in profile. The face in figure 9 is prominent in the middle section and recedes above and below. This is the pure type of *convex form*. The face in figure 10 is prominent above and below, and receding in the middle section. This is the pure type of *concave form*. The face in figure 11 is not particularly prominent in any section but is modelled upon a plane surface. This is the pure type of *plane form*. *Form*, therefore, as used in this science, refers to the contour of the face or of any feature as seen in profile. A convex face has a convex contour. A concave face has a concave contour. A plane face has a plane contour.

While certain forms of features seem to have been evolved along with blondness, and certain other forms along with brunetteness, it is well to bear in mind that every degree and combination of convexity and concavity is to be found associated with every degree of blondness and brunetteness. While it is true, as our statistics prove, that, as a general rule, convex noses and foreheads are found among white peoples, and concave noses and foreheads among dark races, we have seen many examples of concave noses and foreheads among whites, and convex noses and foreheads among dark people. Examples of this are many in any public gathering. One of the most important of all the truths of this science is that any combination of variations of the nine fundamental variables is possible.

THE CONVEX FACE

The significance of the pure convex type is energy, both mental and physical. Superabundance of energy makes the extreme convex keen, alert, quick, eager, aggressive, impatient, positive, and penetrating. As indicated by the form of his forehead, the extreme convex will express his energy in a practical manner — that is to say, in keen

Fig. 10. Dr. T. Alex. Cairns, Lecturer. Pure concave form of profile. Well known for good nature and humour

observation in dealing with material and tangible things. He will demand facts, and will act upon facts quickly and rapidly, being too impatient to wait for reasons and theories and other abstruse considerations which seem to him impractical. The pure convex is not only quick to act but quick to speak. The tendencies indicated by his convex mouth will cause him to speak frankly and at times even sharply and fiercely, without much regard for tact or diplomacy. As indicated by his type of chin, the pure convex is impulsive, expends his energy too rapidly for his limited endurance, and, owing to his lack of self-control and disinclination to deliberate and reason, frequently blunders, and expends his energy uselessly or unprofitably or even harmfully. Being of such a keen, energetic, impatient, practical nature himself, the extreme convex has a stimulating and oftentimes an irritating effect upon others. The impression he makes is always positive, whether that of refreshing frankness and stimulating energy, or offensive sharpness and irritating activity.

THE CONCAVE FACE

The pure concave, as might be expected, is the exact opposite, so far as the indications of form are concerned, of the pure convex. The keynote of his character is *mildness*. His concave nose is an indication of moderate or deficient energy. He is slow of thought, slow of action, patient in disposition, plodding. As indicated by his concave forehead, he thinks far better than he sees or hears, and is therefore liable to fits of absent-mindedness, daydreaming, and meditation. He thinks carefully, seeks out the reasons for things. He is more interested in the reasons for facts than in the facts themselves. His broad, deep, concave chin indicates maturity, self-control, deliberation, slowness to act, determination, and persistence, as well as great powers of mental and physical endurance. His concave mouth indicates a slow, easy, reliable digestion, and, perhaps for that reason, a large freedom from irritability, and consequent tendency to mildness, tactfulness, and diplomacy of speech.

What the convex wins or gains by his aggressiveness, keenness, and superabundance of energy, the concave wins or gains by his diplomacy and unwavering persistence and endurance. Whereas, the effect of the pure convex upon others is positive, and either stimulating or irritating, the effect of the pure concave is negative and soothing, although his extreme deliberation may at times be irritating to the impatient.

Because of his deficient energy, because of his great deliberation, because of his few spoken and written words, and deficiency in self-advertisement,

Fig. 11. Charles Dana Gibson. Pure plane form of profile

because he lacks aggressiveness, the concave is seldom found among men of achievement and prominence. The convex is also, in the majority of cases, a blond. The combination of hopeful, optimistic, restless, organizing, creating, domineering characteristics of the blond with the quick, alert, practical, aggressive qualities of the convex, make this type distinctively the type of action and tangible accomplishment. The concave brunette is an exceedingly rare type among famous men. Whenever one is found he has achieved fame through either philosophy or religion — requiring deep, abstruse thought, or some form of art — requiring years of patient plodding, and detailed, specialized application.

THE PLANE FACE

The individual whose face is modelled upon the plane in form — the plane of his face being parallel with his spinal column — is a balance between the extreme convex and the extreme concave. In this individual we find moderate energy, a type of intellect which, while not so intensely practical as that of the extreme convex, has a good degree of the practical combined with reasonableness and balanced judgment. The plane type has neither the "hair-trigger" impulsiveness of the extreme convex nor the procrastinating deliberation of the extreme concave, but is a balance between the two. The plane, also, is neither extremely quick nor extremely slow, but moderate in his movements and in his thinking. He expresses himself well, and sometimes frankly, but seldom harshly or sharply. He is inclined to be patient, but has decided ideas as to when patience ceases to be a virtue.

Nearly all people approach this balanced or plane type. It is a law established by many experimenters and investigators that the great majority of individuals is to be found at the mean of any variation, and in rapidly decreasing numbers toward the extremes. There are, therefore, among normal white people, a few pure plane, a great many moderately convex, some moderately concave, but relatively few extreme convex, and a still smaller portion of extreme concave. Those who are moderately concave manifest the characteristics of the concave in a moderate degree; those who are moderately convex manifest the characteristics of the convex in moderate degree; and, naturally, the greater the degree of convexity or concavity the greater the degree of the manifestation of their respective characteristics.

As in applying the laws of colour, so in applying those of form it is not difficult for the novice to find *apparent* exceptions. For the trained observer this is not so easy. Exceptions are always merely apparent — never real.

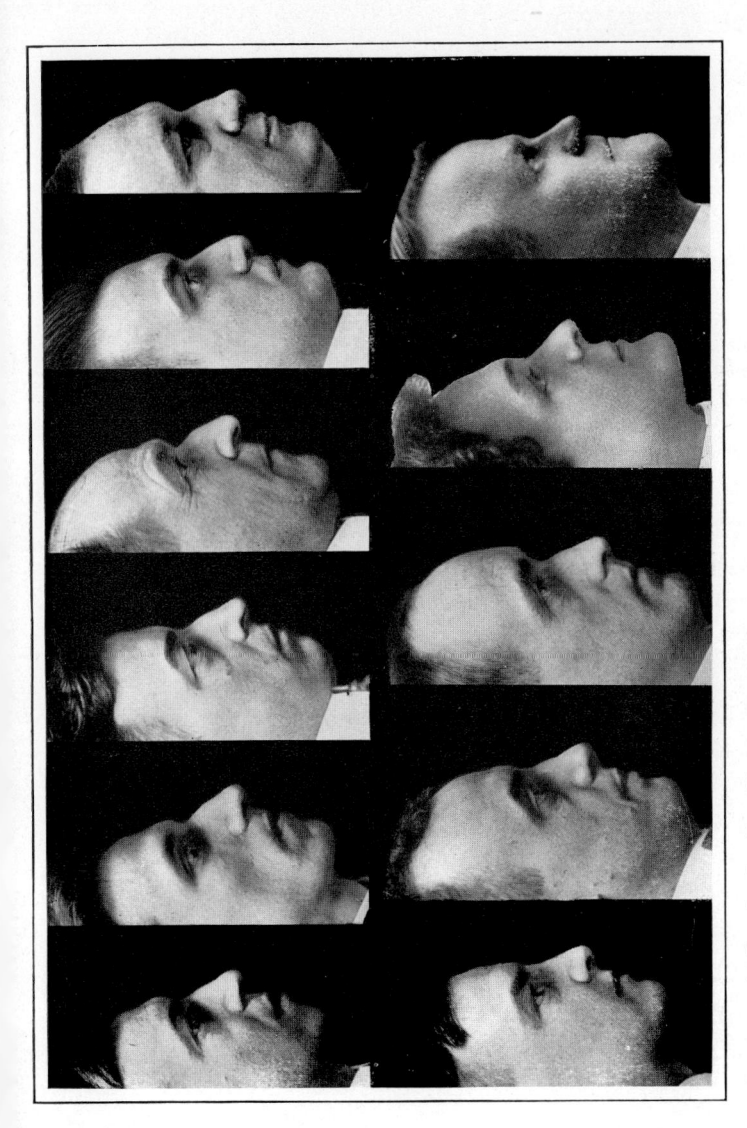

Fig. 12. A Study in Profiles. Beginning at the upper left, which is pure convex, the faces grade into plane at the lower left. Then into pure concave at lower right

ANALYZING THE MAN

Convex features are often associated, in the same face, with concave or plane features. One man may have a convex forehead and nose, and a concave mouth and chin. Another man may have a concave forehead and nose, and a convex mouth and chin. Still another may have concave forehead, mouth, and chin, and convex nose. In all such cases, the interpretation is made by observing the degree of convexity or concavity of each feature, and drawing conclusions based on the evolution of form. Practice is necessary to facility in drawing these conclusions.

SIZE

In treating colour and form we have gone into considerable detail, both as to the evolutionary causes and indications. This has been for the purpose of making clear our method of investigation and method of treatment. While the same methods have been used in studying the other seven variables, perhaps we have made them sufficiently clear and may omit more than a passing mention of causes and indications in this treatise.

Size is one of the most easily observable of all a man's physical attributes, and the place a man should occupy, and the work he can do with relation to his size, ought to be too obvious for comment. It is a fact, however, which any one can demonstrate for himself by visiting any factory, that foremen sometimes put little spiderlike men at work handling big trucks, to the mutual disadvantage of both employer and employee. Tall men are hired to do work that requires constant stooping; short men for jobs where they have to reach up, stretching themselves to the point of discomfort and exhaustion.

In this connection, Frank B. Gilbreth says: "Size of men with relation to their motions has much more influence than is usually realized. Short men are usually the best shovellers where the shovelful need not be raised much in doing the work, such as in mixing mortar and concrete. Few foremen realize that this is because a short man does fewer foot-pounds of work in the same amount of shovelling. On the other hand, when men are shovelling in a trench, the taller the man, usually, the more output per man."* Much stooping or bending soon fatigues a tall man. Reaching for things beyond his height is tiresome to the short man. The tall man with long legs will cover distances or do standing work well. The heavy, vital man must do the bulk of his work while sitting. It is a great mistake to put a heavy man in work which requires him to be much on his feet, unless he is exceptionally well-muscled.

*"Motion Study," page 36.

Photograph by Underwood & Underwood, N. Y.

Fig. 13. Judge Ben. B. Lindsey. A fine example of mental type. Observe triangular face

SIZE AND CHARACTER

The foregoing refers only to the physical considerations of size. The influence of size upon character is readily understood when the intimate relation between muscular action, organic reaction, and emotion is borne in mind. It is a fundamental law of physics that small bodies have less inertia than large — that is to say, they get under way more quickly and move more rapidly in response to the application of the same degree of energy than large bodies. The small man's muscular activities and organic reactions, therefore, are in general quicker and more rapid than the large man's. Granting that Professor James is right in saying that the cause of emotion is physiological, undersized individuals' emotions are more readily and more quickly aroused than the oversized, other things being equal. Pathological conditions may make a small man slow and unresponsive emotionally. Other pathological conditions may make a large man irritable and easily excited, but normally, and in general, our researches have proved that considerations of physiology and psychology are reliable. On the other hand, the law of momentum holds true in this case, and the large man when once aroused is often more intense in his emotions and cools off far more slowly than the small man.

STRUCTURE

The structure of man in general is determined by the relative degree of development and use of three of his chief functional systems — namely, (1) brain and nervous system, (2) muscular and bony system, (3) digestive and nutritive system.

MENTAL TYPE

When the brain and nervous system are most highly developed as the result of both heredity and environment, the head is relatively large in proportion to the body, especially in the upper section, in extreme cases resembling a pear — with the large end up. See figure 13. The bones and muscles are slight and delicate; the features finely chiselled; the shoulders often narrow and sloping; the hair fine in texture, and scanty. Indeed, the general appearance of the extreme type of excessive development of brain and nervous system gives one the impression that the whole physical organism has been subordinated to brain. People of this type have neither the strength nor the endurance for heavy manual labour and, since in addition they are principally interested in intellectual, artistic, literary, scientific, philosophical, and other purely mental subjects, they dislike physical effort, and are discontented and unhappy if obliged to earn their living by manual labour.

Fig. 14. Hon. Wm. G. McAdoo. An example of the motive type

ANALYZING THE MAN

The type, of course, includes several grades of mentality. Merely cataloguing a person in this classification does not mean he is an intellectual giant. If his qualities are moderate, he finds his appropriate niche in some form of clerical work; he is a bookkeeper, a cashier, a stenographer; perhaps a private secretary. If he has more marked talents he may rise to positions that demand the alert, inventive mind; he develops into one of those useful persons recognized as "having ideas." He may be the man whose active suggestions keep the business constantly forging ahead. If he is a lawyer, he is usually the kind known as the "consultant"; he is an expert at writing briefs; knows all the precedents for a hundred years back, and usually furnishes the court the points upon which it decides the case. As a medical man, he is the scientist with eye constantly glued on the microscope. He can discover new things for others to do and even tell how to do them.

THE MOTIVE TYPE

Just as the brain and nervous systems are highly developed by activity, so is the muscular and bony system. The whole make-up of the man who "does things" suggests activity. Muscularity is his predominant physical capital. His face is square rather than triangular. Upon the body there is little surplus flesh. It is broadest at the squarely set shoulders, from which it tapers to the feet. See figure 14 (Hon. Wm. G. McAdoo. An Example of the Motive Type). The key-note of this type of man or woman, boy or girl, is physical activity. They enjoy physical exercise, love the open air, and are well fitted for outdoor pursuits of all kinds. The motive type loves motion, speed, physical contest, movement. Athletes in general, including football players, baseball players, runners, skaters, rowers, pugilists, acrobats, tennis players, and polo players show this type of development. Since they love speed and contest, people of this type should train and drive horses, build and drive automobiles, invent and pilot aeroplanes and motor boats, race on bicycles and motorcycles, and build and operate railroads, factories, dams, canals, bridges, tunnels, buildings of all kinds, ships, and engage in all other phases of active construction and transportation. Since they enjoy and understand motion, people of this type are mechanical. Even babies of motive indications manifest an intense interest in anything that works often before they learn to walk or talk. People of this type, therefore, excel in inventing, designing, building, installing, and operating machinery of all kinds. In short, the motive type is qualified for either directing or performing every kind of physical work and

Fig. 15. Ex-President William H. Taft. A splendid example of the vital type, with judicial aptitudes

activity, including farming, mining, manufacturing, transportation, construction, and exploration.

The natural love of outdoor activity in these people leads them to become soldiers and sailors. All of our great generals and admirals have been pure examples or modifications of this type. Because of their great activity and love of speed and motion, people in whom the bony and muscular system is well developed cannot endure restraint. From loving and demanding physical liberty there is scarcely a step to a love of and demand for civil and religious liberty. This element, therefore, is strong in all martyrs, reformers, great leaders, and pioneers in all kinds of human liberty, and in all ages. Washington, Lincoln, Emerson, Whitman, Luther, Cromwell, Franklin, Wendell Phillips, Garrison, Gladstone, Elbert Hubbard, Roosevelt, and Woodrow Wilson are good examples of modifications of the motive type.

The motive man is just about as ill-fitted to be confined for long hours day after day in an office as the man of extreme intellectual type is for hard, physical work. He demands a considerable amount of physical activity and is neither happy nor healthy unless he gets it. Usually the motive individual is skilful with his hands and fingers. When he is otherwise fitted for it, he produces wonderfully fine needlework, mosaic, jewelry and other similar products. There is a large development of this element in the Chinese, Japanese, and East Indians. The embroideries, laces, hand carvings, mosaics, filigrees, and other objects of art produced by these peoples are famous the world over.

Motive boys and girls are liable to resent the confinement and restraint of school. They are often impatient to leave its mental activities in which they are only mildly interested at best, and begin immediately their active work. The result is that thousands of them forever miss opportunities that might be theirs were they only better educated. They are thus forced to remain for life in subordinate positions, doing mere physical drudgery. Vocational training, giving plenty of opportunity to work with their hands and to develop their inherent mechanical, engineering, or inventive ability, will solve a serious and vital problem for multitudes of boys and girls of this type.

THE VITAL TYPE

When the digestive and nutritive system is most highly developed and most used in proportion to the other organs and functions of the body, the whole person gives evidence of being well nourished. The individual of this type, therefore, has a head comparatively small in proportion to the body; cheeks full and well rounded, giving the face

Fig. 16. Henry Woodruff. An example of fine texture

ANALYZING THE MAN

and head a circular or pear shape — with the big end down (see figure 15); chin full and often double; body modelled upon the circle, large around the waist and tapering to feet and shoulders; limbs round and short; hands and feet well covered with flesh so that the bones and muscles do not show; health usually robust; movement slow and deliberate. The extreme of this type is corpulent. This is the *vital type*.

The predominating characteristic of the vital type is enjoyment of the good things of life. He likes to eat and drink. He loves ease and comfort. Muscular activity is distasteful to him. He often dislikes prolonged, severe mental work. Since vital people do not like to work physically or mentally, and yet crave all of the best products of work, the only way they can gratify their desires is by directing the work of others.

The men who have the natural ability to sit in comfortable chairs and direct the mental and physical activities of thousands of others, reaping for themselves great rewards, are usually of this well-nourished type. Since the vital type is interested in good things to eat, fine and comfortable things to wear, and the comforts and luxuries of life generally, he enjoys handling them and is able to interest other people in them. People of this type are therefore fitted to succeed as butchers, bakers, chêfs, grocers, produce and commission merchants. Modifications of this type are well qualified for the dry goods and clothing business, and indeed for all retail and wholesale merchandising, large and small. Since the handling of money gives a very large degree of control over the activities of other men, and since also money is the medium of exchange for many of the good things of life, the finances of the world are controlled very largely by men of the rounded, well-nourished type. Morgan, Schiff, Stillman, Vanderlip, Ryan, Belmont, Hill, and many other financiers show considerable development of the vital element.

The large man, as we have seen, is slow of movement, with comparatively slow circulation and respiration. It may be for that reason that he is also calm, deliberate, unhurried, and not easily or readily excited. The well-nourished man, other things being equal, is comfortable and free from nervous irritability as well as from apprehension and worry as to his personal well-being. It may be for these reasons that men of this type so often have unprejudiced, judicial minds and are able to weigh all evidence carefully and impartially, and reason to a just and logical conclusion. Well-rounded, full-bodied men are often well fitted to be judges, referees, justices, arbitrators, and in general, to exercise judicial functions.

Fig. 17. Maxim Gorky. An example of coarse texture

ANALYZING THE MAN

Among other good things that men of this type enjoy is a good laugh, and the society and friendship of other people. They are proverbially jolly, good-natured, sociable, friendly, and fond of good stories. They are therefore likely to be successful in politics. If they are writers or speakers they are frequently well known for their wit and humour.

There are all degrees of relative development of brain and nervous system, muscular and bony system, and digestive and nutritive system in individuals. In some, one of these is highly developed and the other two deficient — in others, all three about equally developed. In all cases the characteristics of the three types are shown in direct proportion to the degree of development of each of the three physical systems.

TEXTURE

Texture refers to the degree of fineness or coarseness of fibre or grain in the individual, especially as seen in hair, skin, nails, features, hands, feet, and general body build. Human beings, as can be readily ascertained by casual observation, are coarse or fine in texture, just as fabrics or woods or metals or stones are. According to both biology and embryology, the human brain and nervous system are but specialized inturned skin. The first sign of the nervous system in the scale of evolution is the sensitive cell wall of a one-cell organism. The brain and spinal cord in the human embryo begin in a groove upon the surface, which deepens until it forms a channel, and still further deepens until it becomes a tube. This tube is the embryonic brain and spinal cord. Texture of skin and texture of brain and nervous system are therefore probably related. While the exact nature of brain and nervous function is not known, and there is no scientific evidence that texture of brain and nervous system causes variations in aptitudes, disposition, character, and preferences, extensive investigation and verification, however, have shown that differences in texture of hair, skin, nails, features, hands, and feet, and general body build, are uniformly accompanied by differences in aptitudes, character, and preferences.

The individual of fine texture (see figures 16 and 20) is sensitive and responsive. He loves beauty. He will not work happily and efficiently in coarse, unlovely, harsh surroundings; nor will he be at his best handling coarse, heavy, unbeautiful tools or materials. He likes to do literary, artistic, or scientific work, or to handle fine machinery, beautiful tools, silks and satins, objects of art, jewelry, delicate, light, and artistic work. On the other hand, a man of coarse texture (see figure 17), a man whose hair, skin, features, hands, and body generally, as well as his clothing and manner of speech, all indicate that he is of the "rough and ready" type, and not sensitive, can work happily and efficiently in the midst of dirt and grime. He handles with vigour and effectiveness heavy, unrefined materials and massive machinery.

CONSISTENCY

Under the head of consistency we consider the hardness, softness, or elasticity of bodily tissues. It has never been scientifically demonstrated that natural hardness and density of muscular fibre are associated with relative hardness and density of brain and nerve. However, there are good reasons for supposing that this may be the case.

Physiological psychologists agree that mental and psychical functions and conditions are accompanied by actual physical movements and changes in the brain and nervous structure. That which is hard and dense resists pressure and is slow to change. That which is elastic yields more readily to pressure but springs back when pressure is removed. That which is soft yields readily and quickly to pressure and is easily changed.

Whether or not variations in character are caused by hardness, elasticity, or softness of brain and nervous tissue, extensive observations demonstrate that the man of hard bodily fibre is difficult to impress, unresponsive, slow to change. He is the man who is picturesquely enough called hard-headed and hard-hearted. He does not adapt himself easily to circumstances and conditions. He is, as it were, brittle, and breaks rather than bends or yields. Inasmuch as hard muscles are naturally energetic, the individual of this consistency has hard, relentless, driving, crushing energy.

The individual of elastic consistency of bodily fibre has the same springiness, life, vigour, resilience, and recuperative power which is felt when his hand is grasped. He has normal energy, is adaptable and capable of yielding a point for the sake of harmony. When pressure is removed from him, however, he has a tendency to return to his original state.

The individual of soft consistency is impressionable, easily influenced, vacillating, and, unless braced up from the outside or kept in a sheltered position, is liable to yield to temptation. Such an individual is deficient in energy, does not like hard manual labour and cannot endure hardships. If his softness is so extreme as to be flabbiness, he is a lazy, idle dreamer and easily becomes a chronic invalid.

PROPORTION

Proportion refers to head shape and the relative degree of development of different sections of the

Fig. 18. Theodore Roosevelt in early manhood

Fig. 19. Theodore Roosevelt in middle life. Observe changes in expression

ANALYZING THE MAN

face, head, and body. This variable is subject to most intricate and complex variations which afford more detailed and specific information than the indications of any other variable. For this reason its adequate treatment would be too voluminous for a work of this character.

EXPRESSION

"Normally," says Mantegazza, "every thought and emotion takes form in action. A transitory emotion has a fugitive expression which leaves no trace, but when it is repeated several times it leaves on the face and other parts of the body an expression which may reveal to us a page of the man's history." Since this is true, the careful, studious observer may learn to detect in the expression of people not only their passing, but their permanent, emotions and moods, and learn to recognize the indications of the more subtle.

A marked illustration of the effect of experience and its accompanying emotions and mental processes upon expression is graphically shown in figures 18 and 19, photographs of Theodore Roosevelt, one taken in his early manhood, the other recently. A study of the eyes, mouth, cheeks, and brows will show the increase in concentration, determination, tenacity, intensity, and pugnacity during a few years of the "strenuous life."

Expression shows itself not only in the features, but in every movement, every gesture, the gait, the handshake, the carriage, handwriting, and in many other ways. Everything a man does, says, thinks, or feels is because of the reaction of his particular combination of physical, mental, and psychical traits to external and internal stimuli. Everything he does, therefore, is an indication of his character; and, since, as Mantegazza says, a man's thoughts, feelings, words, and acts, all leave their traces in his face and upon his body, the careful student soon learns to read these signs as one reads a book.

CONDITION

Colour, form, size, structure, texture, consistency, and proportion disclose to the practised eye principally the inherent aptitudes, traits, and characteristics of the individual. Expression indicates to a large extent what the individual has done with his heritage and what life has done to him. The condition of his body, clothing, and personal surroundings indicates his physical and mental habits.

Neat and well-brushed exteriors are not necessarily the signs of marked abilities — some of the ablest men, as we all know, have shamefully neglected their wardrobes — but they do mean that the wearer is painstaking and systematic, and that he possesses a certain degree of self-respect. Carelessness in dress, however, always indicates business laxity. A thrifty housewife reveals the fact in her own appearance as well as in that of her establishment; and a bookkeeper who keeps his clothes well pressed and makes occasional trips to the barber is more likely than not to balance his books. Loud clothes, startling neckties, flamboyant effects in waistcoats and socks, when they are not merely the stigmata of adolescence, mark a man as vain and self-centred.

Condition of body is naturally an excellent indication of the state of health of the individual and reveals much to the practised eye.

CONTRADICTIONS OF NATURAL LAW ONLY APPARENT

These, then, are the nine variables. Each of them is subject to many kinds and degrees of variation, with corresponding variations in character. It is because of the permutation and combination of these variations that billions of human beings — those who have lived on the earth and are living on it to-day — have each his own peculiar appearance and character. There are no duplicates.

A study and observation of any one of the nine variables reveals much in regard to the individual, but it does not reveal all. One of the most difficult of all the obstacles to be overcome by the novice in analysis is the temptation to judge an individual solely by the indications of one variable, or two, or even three. *Everything about a man indicates his character.* Everything is significant. There can be no accurate or reliable analysis unless all nine variables are understood and their significance duly considered. It is perfectly natural that the reader of this chapter should attempt to apply its principles to himself and his friends and acquaintances. In doing so he will doubtless find many apparent discrepancies and contradictions, but these discrepancies and contradictions are only apparent. The laws of human nature, like all other laws of nature, are orderly and uniform in their operation, and do not admit of exceptions. In our own experience every apparent exception has turned out to be either faulty observation or mistaken judgment. A man of scientific mind carefully scrutinizes the evidence, verifies every observation, and examines every link in the chain of his reasoning until he has found everything sound before he reaches his conclusions. Therefore, if he encounters a seeming contradiction of a known law, he does not rest until he has discovered the flaw in either his premises or his conclusion.

One spring, several years ago, we watched the careful researches of a scientist into the physical characteristics of a beautiful lake in Wisconsin.

Fig. 20.   An example of fine texture, concave mouth and chin

Among other things, he learned to his astonishment that the water on the surface of the lake, and for perhaps a few feet below, was several degrees colder than the water in the bottom of the lake. Now, it is a law of physics that the specific gravity of cold water is greater than the specific gravity of warm water. In popular language, cold water is heavier than warm water. Therefore the cold water should have been at the bottom of the lake, and the warm water upon the surface. For a time the scientist was puzzled. Here was an important apparent exception to a known and demonstrable physical law. Carefully and painstakingly the scientist took the temperature readings in all parts of the surface and deeper waters of the lake, verifying his original findings. The results were the same. With equal care he went over every link in his chain of reasoning regarding the phenomenon trying to discover if possible a cause for the seeming contradiction. Finally he told us: "The condition is an unusual one. There has been practically no wind for several days. The lake has no large inlet. Two weeks of low atmospheric temperature, following a month of unusually warm weather, have cooled the surface waters. There being no wind and very little inflowing water to set up currents, the cold water on the top and the warm water underneath are in a state of equilibrium, and until there is some other force applied to set up convection currents this heavy mass of cold water will stand balanced, as it were, upon the lighter mass of warm water underneath. The weather bureau reports fresh southwesterly winds to-morrow, and by to-morrow night I expect to find the cold water at the bottom of the lake and the warm water on the surface. And all day to-morrow you will find strong convection currents flowing upward on the southwest side of the lake, and downward on the northeast side." He was right. The next day he was able to show us by pieces of paper suspended in the water the currents he had promised, while registering thermometers in different parts of the lake indicated that the rest of his predictions had come to pass.

In a similar way, the truly scientific observer of human nature is never disconcerted by any apparent contradictions of its laws, but continues his investigations until he finds out why. The importance of carefully weighing the indications of each of the nine variables, and the significance of their combination in the individual, may be made clear by a chemical analogy.

A CHEMICAL ANALOGY

A student of chemistry may learn all the characteristics of oxygen, carbon, and hydrogen, but he may know nothing of the attributes of their many compounds until he has learned the significance of their combination in different proportions. Just as all human beings exhibit combinations of the nine variables mentioned, so all carbohydrates are combinations of oxygen, hydrogen, and carbon. Just as carbon, oxygen, and hydrogen in one compound give us fiery, poisonous carbolic acid, and in different proportions sweet, healing honey, so the nine elements combined in certain proportions may make of one man a degenerate, thief, and murderer, and of another man a patriotic and philanthropic citizen.

The analogy may be carried even further. Oxygen is a gas lighter than air, colourless, slightly acid in odour and taste. Hydrogen is also a gas very much lighter than air, colourless, odourless, and tasteless. Carbon is a solid, and usually hard, dense, and black. None of the characteristics of any of these three elements is to be found in butter, molasses, phenacetin, or oil of peppermint. Yet these three, and these three only, are in the substances named.

In a similar way, combinations of the nine elements of human character in different proportions yield characteristics not indicated by any one of the nine. For example, a man's honesty, his disposition to loyalty, his industry, his carefulness, his conscientious accuracy, and many other such qualities cannot be determined by an observation of any one of these nine variants alone, but can be unerringly appraised by careful observation and analysis of the proportions in which the qualities indicated by the nine elements are combined.

It is abundantly clear, from the foregoing, that the character analyst who attempted to judge of the qualifications of any applicant for a position merely because he was of fine texture and blond complexion, would go as far wrong as a chemist who analyzed a carbohydrate quantitatively for carbon and hydrogen, but neglected to do more than determine the presence of oxygen.

Camphor and olive oil have approximately the same proportion each of carbon and hydrogen, but because of a slight difference in proportion of oxygen, and in the manner of their combination, one is aromatic, strong to the taste, and poisonous, while the other is mild, soothing, and nourishing.

So two men may be almost exact counterparts of each other in texture, size, form, colour, and consistency, but on account of a difference in proportion, expression, and condition, one will be a lazy, shiftless, careless, irresponsible burden upon society, and the other a successful financier.

CHAPTER IX

ANALYZING THE MAN — PRACTICAL APPLICATION

THERE ought to be a high membership ideal for every plant, no newcomer admitted who is not fit in every way, no man cut off except for cause. . . . If it is a duty to exclude the morally unfit, it is also a duty to exclude more vigorously from any particular occupation those who are congenitally unfitted to make a success of it. A blind man may become a self-supporting, useful, and successful member of society; a man born without legs may become the successful owner and operator of a livery stable, driving, harnessing, and unharnessing horses; but a blind man cannot act as lookout on an ocean steamer, the deaf man cannot lead an orchestra, and the legless man cannot become a foot racer." — HARRINGTON EMERSON.[*]

In applying character analysis to the problems of employment the ideals are: First, to ascertain the health, aptitudes, traits, tendencies, disposition, character, habits, training, and experience of

[*] "Twelve Principles of Efficiency," pages 154-5.

each applicant as expeditiously and easily as possible; second, to verify, check up, and compare all available data in such a way as to leave the least possible probability of error; third, to record the results of this observation and analysis in permanent form for future guidance and comparative study. That these ideals may be realized we have devised and, after much experimentation, brought to their present form the Analysis Blank shown on page 86 and the Application Blank shown on pages 82 and 83.

THE ANALYSIS BLANK

When this blank has been filled out by a competent examiner, any other worker in the employment department who understands the cipher gleans from it such an accurate mental picture of the applicant that, in many cases, he could very easily pick him out of a crowd. In this respect, it somewhat resembles the *portrait parle* or "word picture" devised by Bertillion, by means of which an expert recognizes the subject even more surely than he could by means of a photograph. As will be seen, the space for conclusions gives the widest possible latitude to the interviewer. It is to be filled out according to the class and type of applicant, the position he is to take, the character of his future activities, and any other pertinent considerations.

ANALYZING THE MAN

This blank provides for the observation in the applicant of each of the nine variables. Colour is observed in the hair, eyes, skin, and beard, since in detailed analysis each has its significance. Form also is observed in the eyes, nose, mouth, and chin. The relative degree of development of the mental, motive, and vital elements is indicated; as are also texture and consistency. The capacity of intellect is an important observation. A good employment expert knows better than to recommend a man for a position for which he has either too great or too little intelligence. Proportion, expression, and condition of body and dress are each recorded.

When the interviewer has reached his conclusion, he sets down the applicant's strongest and best qualities, listed here as positives; also his weakest qualities, listed here as negatives. There are certain negatives which handicap a man for any work, and it is necessary to keep a record of these when they are found, and of the degree of deficiency in each case.

Under "recommendations" the interviewer states his best judgment as the result of his observations of and conversation with the applicant, taking into consideration not only his record upon the analysis blank, but also the information given by the applicant himself upon the application blank, and what is revealed in his interview.

CHECKING AND COMPARING DATA

In arriving at the conclusions entered upon the analysis blank, much valuable data are obtained from the application blank, and from the responses of the applicant to the questions on the reverse of it. These questions bring out, indirectly, information by which the interviewer's observations may be verified — or modified, as the case may be. Just at this point it hardly seems necessary to state that no applicant is asked to write anything or answer any question if he shows any disinclination to do so. It is the purpose of this plan to avoid as far as possible anything that savours of the third degree, grilling the applicant, asking him embarrassing questions, prying into his private affairs, or otherwise alarming or offending him. As a general rule, we have found that when kindly treated, applicants willingly fill out these blanks and answer all questions.

Studied in the light of experience and knowledge, this application blank reveals much. The manner in which the applicant answers the questions put to him by the interviewer is carefully noted and considered. When a man writes his name, address, and other items, he tells far more about himself than he thinks. Like voice, handwriting is an expression of character. Among other indications, a man's writing shows his expertness with a pen.

While this is not always essential, yet well-trained fingers show at least latent ability to handle small tools of any kind. The rapidity with which he fills in the blank will indicate, to some degree, his quickness of thought.

It is obviously important to have the applicant's name. Aside from this, there is much in a name. As a general rule, a man has no choice in the matter of his name. He may receive from his parents by inheritance and by gift the appellative John Smith, or he may be more gaudily decorated with Reginald Algernon de la Rey. But the one may appear in after life as Ivan Smyth, and the other as R. A. Delarey. The man who was known to the world as Grover Cleveland was named Stephen Grover Cleveland by his parents, and Woodrow Wilson began life as Thomas Woodrow Wilson.

Nationality: However much we wish it otherwise, race and national prejudices and hatreds are significant, fundamental, and stubborn facts. Even those from different sections of the same country are often antagonistic and will not work well together. It is dangerous to place north Italians and south Italians in the same gang. Germans and Englishmen do not harmonize readily, nor do Irishmen and negroes. An acquaintance with international affinities and enmities will be a great help in placing men.

Religion: In the same way, and for the same reason, it is often desirable to know the religion of the applicant. Roman Catholics will work best under a foreman of their own belief. In no case is it wise to place in charge of others any man who makes himself obnoxious because of his intense religious beliefs. Both national feeling and religion are products of the emotions. Emotions when aroused are like dynamite — dangerous explosives. Frank B. Gilbreth says: "A bond of sympathy between the workmen and the people who are to occupy the edifice upon which they are working will also increase the output."*

Date of Birth: Many firms make it a hard-and-fast rule not to employ men beyond a certain age. Years are not always the test of a man's age. Youthfulness is of the spirit and is not measured by calendars and birthdays. The man who looks young for his years is usually advancing. He who looks older than he should is slipping backward.

Height and Weight: The height and weight of men in connection with their work should also be considered. See page 159.

Single or Married: Happily married men, other things being equal, do the best work. They are more permanent. Bachelors come next. The man with serious domestic trouble is least efficient and

*"Motion Study," page 15.

ANALYZING THE MAN

least satisfactory of all. Therefore, in selecting men for important positions, it is an essential to know something of their domestic relations. This is not difficult to ascertain by indirect methods if the interviewer is tactful and sympathetic. A man's ambitions for his home and for permanent employment throw light on his family relations. The man may be single yet have a large family dependent upon him; hence the next inquiry.

Ever Employed Here: If a man has been employed by the firm before, and there is an adequate system of records, it will be possible to learn how he performed. Under this plan there will be complete data concerning him. In the absence of such information, it is important to know why he left and why he wishes to return.

Position Wanted: The applicant may be applying for a position far beneath his abilities — or far beyond them. Or he may be applying for work in one department when his talents fit him especially for another. The interviewer should discover such errors by weighing the evidence with the requirements of the position in mind.

Permanent or Temporary: It is also for the interviewer to determine whether this is a "temporary" man seeking a permanent position, or not.

Positives and Negatives: Perhaps no part of this blank has aroused greater curiosity or more comment than the list of "positives" and "negatives." The head of a prominent employment agency was moved almost to tears in his pity for our innocence and credulity in making this list a part of our blank. "Why!" he mourned, "any man would lie on a proposition of that kind. He wants the job and is willing to do anything to get it. Naturally he will put his best foot forward and hand himself every positive quality on the list. You never can find out anything about men that way."

This list of positives and negatives is not submitted to applicants for the purpose of obtaining direct information from them. The man who calmly and without hesitation assigns to himself all the desirable qualities and none of the undesirable, gives to the trained observer just as valuable and just as accurate information about himself as does the man who painstakingly, with much introspection and an excess of truthfulness, checks the good qualities he thinks he possesses in sufficient degree to entitle him to credit for them, and such bad qualities as he considers himself guilty of, or the man who scratches his head, hesitates, and doubts his ability to check them correctly. It is also an interesting fact that the man who takes the most pains to be honest in checking up this list oftentimes gives us far less reliable information, so far as his check marks are concerned, than does the

ANALYZING THE MAN

man who nonchalantly accredits himself with all the virtues.

Not infrequently it happens that an applicant in all honesty credits himself with positives he does not possess, and charges himself with negatives utterly foreign to his nature. In short, the important feature of this part of the application blank is not the positives or the negatives checked but the *reaction of the applicant* to this list.

It is a simple and easy enough deduction that the man who swiftly and cheerfully strings a row of marks alongside the positive qualities is of somewhat easy conscience and willing to take chances; that the man who painstakingly and carefully checks some positives and some negatives is careful, conscientious, conservative, cautious, and somewhat inclined to be slow and deliberate. The man who too easily checks all of the negatives is either a hypocrite or is lacking in self-appreciation. The man who credits himself with good qualities, and charges himself with bad qualities erroneously, is either wanting in introspection, simply careless, or has ideals so high that one departure from perfection causes him to count himself lacking.

Some applicants are simply appalled at this list. "Why," they say, "I haven't any idea how to check myself. I don't even know how to begin. I don't know about myself. I would rather you'd hire me and find out." Others ask for counsel in checking the list.

Thus in many ways applicants reveal in some measure their characters, their aptitudes, and their habits as they react to this list of positives and negatives. A good example of this is to be found in the autobiographies of great men, particularly scientists, engineers, and scholars. Sir Francis Galton, Prof. Simon Newcomb, Sir Henry Bessemer, and Cardinal Newman told the truth about themselves in their autobiographies. Cellini's autobiography is a good example of the opposite type. He was an artist but a braggart, and his autobiography teems with self-praise.

NOT ALL APPLICANTS QUESTIONED

It would seem that any person of ordinary intelligence would know that these questions are suggested to the employment supervisor and his assistants merely as a guide and not as a hard-and-fast schedule. And yet we have been most entertainingly pictured as inquiring of an Italian immigrant seeking a position as wielder of pick and shovel: "In school what study did you like best?" and "If you could have any position you wished for, what would it be?" When we devised these questions, as the result of many years' experience, we did so in the hope that those who used them in examining

ANALYZING THE MAN

applicants would do so with common sense. We have not been disappointed.

Two of the questions we ask, when their use is indicated, are these: "What kind of work do you like best?" and "If you could have any position you wished for, what would it be?" It is expected that these questions should be used in examining young men, to ascertain whether or not they have any well-defined idea as to what they wish to become. They are to be asked after the interviewer has established relations of fullest confidence with the applicant, so that he is thoroughly at his ease and willing to talk about his ambitions. A man's ideal is the most important thing about him. It does more to determine his value and ultimate success than any other one element in his character. Some men, however, tell us of their great ambition, and yet apply for a job that does not lead toward it. There is a vast difference between mere, limp wishing and strong, definite purpose. Occasionally a man seeks a position seemingly inconsistent with his ideals but really bearing directly upon their realization. A man who is ambitious as a writer on economics for business men once sought a position as salesman that he might learn something about the economics of distribution. His ambition was perfectly legitimate, but under the circumstances it was not deemed advisable to spend the time and money necessary to train and prepare him merely for temporary work as salesman.

In a similar way, each of the questions suggested, when wisely put and its answer intelligently interpreted, is of great value.

DEALING WITH UNTRUTHFULNESS

In putting these questions and all others to applicants, it is always to be borne in mind that many men, through ignorance or bad training or unfortunate environment, are untruthful. Perhaps one of the most potent causes of this untruthfulness, especially among less intelligent workmen, is that they have been so discourteously and brutally treated by some employers that they think they are obliged to lie in order to secure employment. While at first it is necessary for an employment supervisor and his staff to be on their guard lest they be deceived, experience has abundantly shown that kind treatment, justice, and patient instruction soon make most of these men fairly reliable and many of them trustworthy. Until such results are obtained, however, methods must be used which will ascertain the truth. And the only safe, effective method known to us is careful, intelligent observation of external signs which the man can neither change nor conceal — in fact, which he does not even know can be observed.

Many foreigners, new to our ways, give to their employers so many different names that it is sometimes a question whether some of them know what their true names are. It is no uncommon thing for a labourer, discharged from one department in the morning, to apply for work in another department by a different name in the afternoon. Where there are day and night gangs we have known men to work in the day gang by one name, and in the night gang by another. "When do they sleep?" you ask. During the time they are supposed to be at work. One such versatile fellow, a Syrian, seemed absolutely unable to understand that he had done any wrong in making such an arrangement.

ABOUT PSYCHOLOGICAL TESTS

We have frequently been asked whether we use psychological tests. Where undesirable publicity has made a feature of the analysis work of an employment department it is difficult enough to allay the suspicions of the average applicant and get him to fill out an application blank. One can imagine what it would be like to get his sincere coöperation in a series of elaborate psychological tests. Furthermore, we have faithfully tried many psychological tests and have found either that it was so difficult to maintain ideal conditions that the results were negative and unreliable, or that when the results were reliable they could have been far more easily obtained by observation.

But, even granting that psychological tests were easily applied, that they were reliable and gave information not otherwise obtainable, no psychological tests have yet been devised to determine a man's honesty, his good nature, his industry, his cheerfulness, his courtesy, or any one of many other most important qualifications. There are some positions where tests of hearing and vision are necessary, and in these cases we use them. But for practically all other aptitudes, and for all traits of character, we repeat, the only safe and effective method is trained observation.

DRAWING CONCLUSIONS

The practical and perhaps the most difficult part of our problem confronts us when, having completed our analysis of the man, we undertake to fit him to his job. In the solution of this part of our problem the best possible guide is common sense enlightened by intelligently interpreted experience.

There are many factors in this problem. Here are the analyses of the different jobs in the organization, each with its physical, intellectual, and psychical requirements. Here is the analysis of the man, showing his physical, intellectual, and psychical qualifications. Here are the requisitions for

ANALYZING THE MAN

men from executives, showing which of the positions in the organization are available. A process of elimination rapidly narrows the choice down to a very few. If the man is a pronounced blond, then all positions requiring close application, sustained activity, slow, plodding, patient effort are eliminated. If the man is concave in form, then all those positions requiring aggressiveness, keenness, alertness, energy, and a sense of the practical are dropped from consideration. If the man is small in size, then all those positions requiring slow, powerful, rhythmical action are out of the question. If the applicant is of very fine texture, then all positions in harsh, unlovely environment, which require handling heavy, coarse materials or tools, and constant association with those of coarse texture and crude manners will not fit. If the applicant is of hard consistency, then positions requiring sympathy, gentleness, and adaptability are unfitted for his type. If the applicant lacks endurance or carefulness or ambition or courage, or any of the qualities indicated by variations in proportion, then positions requiring the exercise of these qualities must be eliminated. If the applicant's expression shows him to be pessimistic, then any position which requires hopefulness and cheerfulness is not for him. If the applicant's condition of body and dress show him to have careless, slack, slovenly habits, then any position requiring neatness, accuracy, order, cleanliness, and careful attention to details must be excluded. Constant practice soon enables the employment supervisor and his assistants to make these eliminations quickly — almost instantaneously. In fact, while reading about it may make the operation of this plan seem slow and cumbersome, in actual practice it is swift and convenient.*

*The report of the employment department in the —— company for January, 1913, indicates the amount of work that can be done by a small force under this plan. During this month, in addition to the employment supervisor, there were two interviewers for shop applicants, one interviewer for office applicants, and one stenographer in the department. The following is the record:

	For Shop	For Offices	Total
Interviewed	1,601	391	1,992
Applications taken in office	294	137	431
Referred to foremen	299	84	383
Rejected by foremen	5	0	5
Rejected by employment department	231	74	305
Hired	277	85	362
Removed from pay-roll	317	23	340
Transferred	206	37	243
Rates changed	150	48	198
Applications by mail			231
Rejections by mail			49

It may be said in explanation of these figures that the employment department in this company had been installed but a comparatively short time. Extensive reconstruction and reorganization had been begun before the installation of the department, owing to the introduction of efficiency standards, a change from piece rates to the bonus system of payment, and other causes. For these reasons the number removed from the pay-roll, transferred, and changed in rate is very high. However, only six months earlier, before reorganization and reconstruction were begun, and when there was no employment department, the number removed from the pay-roll every month averaged 550. In order to maintain the force an equal number were hired each month. Therefore, even under the stress of sweeping changes in policy and methods, for which it was not responsible, the employment department was able to reduce the number of monthly changes in the pay-roll more than 30 per cent.

ANALYZING THE MAN

The process of elimination having greatly simplified the problem, it remains to determine for which of the few available positions the applicant is best fitted. If the applicant is of moderate natural abilities and attainments, and the available positions are comparatively simple in their requirements, the problem is not a difficult one. When, however, the applicant is a man of unusual ability, either latent or highly developed, and there are vacancies with high requirements, the fitting of the man to his job often calls for a high degree of intelligence and judicial capacity. Then it is that many of the refinements of analysis and a careful interpretation of the significance of the combination of the nine variables in the individual come into play.

HOW THE PLAN WORKS

To many who pride themselves on being "practical" this no doubt seems theoretical and futile. There is a feeling on the part of many able employers that there is a subtle something about human beings that defies analysis, and that the most carefully planned and executed system of analysis is more likely than not to miss altogether, while the practical man who relies on his intuition makes a good choice more frequently than does the scientific analyst. Such a feeling is perfectly natural and justifiable. Any mere theoretical system based upon one or two or even four or five variables would thus come to grief when put to the test. But a system of analysis based not upon theory but worked out as the result of years of practical experience, and taking into consideration not a few things, but everything about a man, simply utilizes scientifically the substance of the practical man's intuitions, as he calls them, and in addition a great deal of organized, classified, and verified knowledge.

Those who make careful use of this plan may, and do, make occasional blunders, but they are not guilty of glaring ones in fitting the man to his job and to his environment. They do not place a nervous, high-strung, sensitive, temperamental man under a harsh, loud-voiced, unsympathetic, hard, driving, superior executive. Since they can easily determine the degree and quality of an applicant's honesty, they have never yet given a gambler, a man of great shrewdness and cunning, with a passion for money, deficient conscience, and weak will, or a plain, deliberate crook, charge of cash. They do not send a lazy, apathetic, unsociable, and easily discouraged man out on the road as salesman. They do not recommend the employment of crude, coarse-textured, rough and ill-mannered men for positions where they come constantly in contact with a discriminating public. They do not put a restless, volatile, eager, liberty loving, and intensely active individual into a job which ties him down to a careful handling of minute details, monotonous routine, and exasperating annoyances. They do not recommend as an executive a man of weak personality or deficient sense of justice or unreliable temper or a disagreeable aloofness of manner. Perhaps it is not too much to say that selections very much like these are not altogether unknown where "practical" methods are in use.

Character analysis by the observational method is not infallible; nor can it ever be infallible so long as its conclusions must rest upon the fallible observations and judgment of mere human beings. But in so far as observation can be trained by practice, and in so far as judgment can be enlightened by knowledge and experience, to just that degree can the science of character analysis by the observational method be made a safe, sane, practical basis for the selection, assignment, management, and education of employees.

CHAPTER X

THE BOSS

"I do not like thee, Dr. Fell.
The reason why I cannot tell.
But this I know, and know full well,
I do not like thee, Dr. Fell.

THE old rhyme expresses a common human experience. We all have our likes and our dislikes. We are attracted to some people and repelled by others. We naturally harmonize with some and are in a state of constant friction and discord with others.

This principle of attraction or repulsion, harmony or discord operates not only among human beings but is universal. Watch your dog as he follows you on a tramp into the country. Notice his behaviour with the other dogs he meets. As soon as he sees some dogs his tail begins to wag and within a few minutes they are friendly. He approaches other dogs growling, with his teeth showing and his hair bristling. Observe carefully and you will see the same likes and dislikes among horses, cats, birds, and even insects.

The principle holds good in inanimate nature. Some chemicals have a powerful affinity for each other. Others are utterly unresponsive. Still others are dangerous and explosive when brought together. Musical tones may produce harmony or discord.

There are some likes and dislikes of ours that we can explain. We dislike this man because he is narrow and bigoted, and that man because he is a braggart. We like one of our friends because he is good-natured and diplomatic, and another because he is charmingly deferential and courteous. But many of our likes and dislikes are mysteries. They are cases of Dr. Fell.

In a similar way, the uninformed man does not understand the attractions and repulsions among animals. He does not know just why chemicals react to one another so differently. And he can give no satisfactory explanation of the reasons for harmony and discord in musical tones.

But, if the layman does not know why musical tones produce harmony or discord, the musician does. If the man in the street does not know why chemicals behave toward one another as they do, the chemist does. In like manner, if you cannot tell why you do not like Dr. Fell, the thoughtful observer and student of human nature can. If he has seen both you and Dr. Fell, he knows before you meet that you will not like the Doctor.

ANALYSIS REVEALS CAUSES OF INHARMONY

These phenomena of harmony and inharmony are not accidents or coincidences. In a universe where law is supreme nothing just happens. For every effect there must be an adequate cause. Since there are causes for likes and dislikes, analysis can hunt them out, classify them, note their indications, and safely predicate their operation. With a knowledge of such causes, the observer and thinker can work out a table of affinities as complete, although perhaps not so definite and exact, as a table of chemical affinities.

The practical value of such knowledge in employment is obviously great. So little are the perfectly natural causes of harmony and discord between individuals understood that we blame the man who cannot get along with his superior, or perhaps the superior who is always having trouble with his men. It is perfectly human and largely excusable for an executive to think that the employee he dislikes is inefficient, insolent, and insubordinate, or that in some other perfectly indefensible way he is to blame. And it is just as human and just as excusable for the employee to believe that the boss he can't get along with "has it in for him," is jealous of him, won't give him a fair deal, and is ignorant, unjust, and incompetent. No one knows better than the employer how distressing and wasteful are these feuds between executives, great and small, and their men.

DESTRUCTIVE EFFECT OF INHARMONY

Few conditions throw sand into the bearings of an industrial or commercial machine like inharmony. The least of all wastes due to this cause is the inability of the executive to arouse and inspire to superior efforts the man who hates or despises him. Worse than this are the slackening bonds of discipline, the stirring up of negative, destructive thoughts and feelings in both superior and subordinate, the waste of energy in friction, misunderstandings, and other causes of inefficiency. Even worse in some respects than these effects is the fact that the institution is being continually drained of valuable human assets. If the executive dislikes a man he eventually discharges him, and, by an unwritten law in most institutions, that man cannot after that be employed in any department. And yet every employer knows full well that many a valuable man has been lost in this way. It is for this very reason that executives, otherwise all but impossible, have sometimes been retained in the service because they have the faculty of tying their men together and to themselves with cords of unbreakable loyalty.

As this is being written, a great and disastrous

strike is in progress in some English cotton mills as the result of friction between a foreman and his subordinates. Every close student of industrial history knows that such strikes are by no means infrequent. The average employer throws his human chemicals together at random. He has no idea, until he tries them out, whether they will mingle in an efficient compound, or neutralize each other and become inert, or form a corrosive poison that will eat the vitals out of his business, or explode and blow the whole organization into pieces so scattered that they are difficult to reassemble.

WHO IS THE BOSS?

The properly qualified and trained employment supervisor, having determined the right man for the right job, assigns him to the right boss. In this classification, the word "boss" is used to designate the man's immediate superior, whether he be general manager, manager, superintendent, department manager, chief clerk, head bookkeeper, principal, foreman, gang-boss, or any other executive. This is the boss with whom the man must work — must coöperate. The word boss, therefore, refers to the individual executive as distinct from the management.

There are many elements to be considered in the relationship between the man and the boss, between the boss and his men. We have mentioned harmony, which is one of the most important if not the most important. Harmony between the man and the boss depends upon many things — among them the proportion and nature of positive and negative elements of character in each. An extremely positive boss will not work harmoniously with extremely positive or extremely negative men, and conversely. This fact will be readily recognized by any observant employer by a study of the following analysis of the two types:

POSITIVE — OR DRIVING	NEGATIVE — OR DRAWING
Keen	Mild
Quick	Deliberate
Domineering	Persuasive
Changeable	Constant
Impatient	Patient
Opinionated	Teachable
Excitable	Calm

The positive, driving type, if given men of his own degree of positiveness, will arouse antagonism and insubordination. The negative type, if given men of his own disposition, will fail to arouse enthusiasm and stimulate action. Give the positive boss men several degrees more negative than himself, and the negative boss men several degrees more positive than himself, and the result is harmony.

One of the very best workmen we have ever known, a man in whom the characteristics classified as "negative" predominated, we found suffering in his accustomed silence under the stinging taunts of an executive of the extreme positive type. And the executive was suffering almost as much as his subordinate at the man's extreme deliberation. His calm, unruffled temper, his careful, methodical ways drove his high-strung, erratic, excitable boss almost to distraction. Upon our recommendation, this man was transferred to a boss only a little more positive than himself. The workman and both bosses were delighted with the change, and a valuable man almost lost by discharge was saved to the institution.

Another frequent cause of serious trouble is difference in degree of sensitiveness. The extremely fine-textured, responsive individual often finds the tactlessness and lack of delicacy of the coarse textured almost intolerable.

SOME CAUSES OF INHARMONY AND THE METHOD OF CURE

Narrow, bigoted, egotistical, and self-assertive men will invariably clash. Each wants to be right all the time and each takes the opposite view from the other as a matter of course. The boss who is deficient in sense of humour utterly fails to understand and cannot endure the pleasantries of a subordinate who is full of jokes and pranks. The man of dignity, seriousness, and solemnity is always annoyed by flippancy or a tendency to chaffing, especially on the part of subordinates. A college president with no tolerance for student pranks is a good example.

Experience teaches the observant that differences in nationality, in religion, in race, in various local allegiances, and in other matters often render the man and his boss incompatible. The boss whose one idea is work, hard, unrelenting, never-tiring work, often doing things in the hardest possible way, will not understand or tolerate the man whose ideal is efficiency, who seeks the best, easiest, and quickest ways — with sufficient periods of relaxation. There are many possible causes of friction and misunderstanding — more than could be enumerated. They depend somewhat upon the nature of the business, the character of employees, and the locality. It is the employment supervisor's duty to study these and learn to provide against them in the assignment of employees to foremen and other executives.

The same considerations apply to a certain extent to the association of employees together.

The relationship between the man and his boss is one of the most important as well as the most difficult of all the factors in the employment problem. One executive whose records we examined produced 62 units a week with a force of 122 men. His successor, under precisely the same conditions, and with the same grade of men, produced 123 units a week with 39 men — a net increase in efficiency of 620 per cent. In another case, a good executive increased the output 163 per cent. when given a force of men who were suited to his type. The increase in harmony and in the quality of product was even greater, though not measurable in percentages. These examples are typical.

No hard and fast rules for the solution of this problem can be laid down. Knowledge of human nature, sympathy, keen observation, alertness to conditions, careful study of compatibilities, sane common sense, sound, logical reasoning, good judgment, and singleness of purpose on the part of both management and employment department are the best guarantee of efficient assignment of men and bosses.

The practical procedure of this feature of the work of the employment department is comparatively simple. As rapidly as possible, the employment supervisor interviews every executive in the organization. In these interviews many subjects are discussed, bringing out various points of view, prejudices, and idiosyncrasies of the executives. The real purpose of the interview, although they may not know it, is to give the employment supervisor an opportunity to make a careful analysis, and thus to determine their characters and dispositions. In these interviews employment supervisors have found executives who frankly stated that they would not tolerate Germans. Others have confessed a similar prejudice against negroes, Poles, Italians, Irishmen, etc. Frequently executives are found who prefer men of some one nationality. Some bosses prefer blonds; others prefer brunettes. A little tact and patience brings out all these preferences.

SOME SAMPLE ANALYSES

As the employment supervisor interviews and analyzes each executive he makes notes which are afterward crystallized into detailed and definite instructions for his own guidance and the guidance of each member of his staff, telling the kind of men preferred by each executive as well as the pet aversions of each.

The following sample instructions taken from the records of an employment department show how this is done:

FOUNDRY

Assistant Superintendent — A.——
  Requirements for men:
    Quickness
    Energy

Will get along well with almost any man.
Prefers Poles; second, Italians.
Thinks Greeks too good for foundry work.

PRODUCTION DEPARTMENT

Foreman — W. L. ——
  Requirements for men:
    Quickness
    Keenness
    Accuracy
    Obedience
    Good nature
    Not too great sensitiveness.

DRILL PRESS DEPARTMENT

Foreman — H. ——
  Requirements for men:
    Obedience
    Teachableness
    Steadiness
    English-speaking Poles, English-speaking Hungarians, but no Syrians, Italians, or other foreigners.
    Inexperienced farmer boys preferred.

SCREW MACHINE DEPARTMENT

Foreman — A. S. ——
  Requirements for men:
    Youth
    Medium height
    Muscular build
    Americans preferred.

PLANER AND SHAPER DEPARTMENTS

Foreman — A. ——
  Requirements for men:
    Stocky, muscular build

THE BOSS

Brunette colour
Germans or Poles preferred
Apprentices about 18 years old to start on drill presses.

TURRET LATHE DEPARTMENT

Foreman — M. ——   (Speaks German)
  Requirements for men:
  Slowness
  Calmness
  Dependableness
  Carefulness
  Patience
  For larger machines, should weigh about 160 lbs.
  For smaller machines, should weigh about 135 lbs.
  Prefers Americans.

TRUCKING DEPARTMENT

Foreman — H. G. ——
  Requirements for men:
  Physical strength
  Good sense of location
  Good sense of direction
  Good memory
  Americans or foreigners intelligent enough to read and write English

ERECTING DEPARTMENT

Foreman — Z. ——
  Requirements for men:
  Dependableness
  Slowness
  Steadiness
  Reliability
  Brunette colour
  (Doesn't like nervous men).

IMPORTANCE OF THE BOSS

One of the most heart-breaking phases of employment work is the spending of time and money in securing, analyzing, selecting, and assigning valuable employees, only to see them spoiled and their usefulness to the organization all but ruined by an incompetent boss. This, too, is often one of the most difficult problems to solve. Business institutions are not ideal. Perhaps there are good reasons why conditions which seem ideal from the point of view of employment are not ideal measures of business expediency. Whatever the cause, it is often impossible to replace every undesirable and incompetent executive with a desirable one. In such cases the employment supervisor must make the best of the situation — assigning employees with all the wisdom at his command. Here, however, is a situation which will repay the most earnest study on the part of any management which protects and sustains, for any reason, executives who have a record of frequent changes in the personnel of their departments, and complain that their work suffers because they cannot secure or keep good men.

However needful to select efficient employees for the rank and file, it is far more needful to place good men and women in authority, high and low. An efficient executive can secure good results from mediocre men; but an incompetent executive will nullify the ability of the best of men. Napoleon's victory at Austerlitz was not because he had superior troops — nor was his defeat at Waterloo due to inferior soldiers. Alexander's thirty thousand at Issus were no better men than Darius' million — the difference was between Napoleon in 1805 and Napoleon in 1815 — between Alexander and Darius.

CHAPTER XI

THE EMPLOYMENT SUPERVISOR AND HIS STAFF

THE success of any employment plan depends largely upon the aptitudes, character, and training of the employment supervisor. A competent supervisor, well qualified for his work by character and disposition, makes a fair success even with a poor plan. A supervisor unfitted for his work cannot succeed even with the best plan that could be devised. In choosing an employment supervisor we seek first of all one who *understands people*, sympathizes with them, and truly loves his fellow-men.

UNDERSTANDING OF HUMAN NATURE

Some people are naturally good judges of human nature. These can easily acquire the scientific training necessary to convert fairly accurate guesses into definite knowledge. We have selected and installed employment supervisors who, within six months, had so far supplemented their natural gifts with special training as to make them excellent judges of aptitudes and character. The man who understands people usually sympathizes with and loves them. Because he loves to deal with them and to come in contact with them, he is efficient and successful.

SYMPATHY

We have looked on in admiration at the *kindliness*, *tact*, and *sympathy* of a young employment supervisor of but four or five months' experience as he dealt with the complicated situations brought before him for adjustment. His calm, unruffled, gentle demeanour, his quick understanding of motives and emotions, and his scientific knowledge as to how to deal with them straightened out tangles and hard knots and adjusted differences and difficulties.

An employment supervisor of this kind sets the pace for his entire staff and is himself the spirit of his entire department. The moment an applicant or employee enters such a department he feels that he is among those who understand him and who are his friends. Not only employees in the rank and file, but foremen, heads of departments, and even higher executives soon get into the habit of going to such an employment supervisor, not only in the regular routine of business, but for counsel, encouragement, and assistance in solving their problems.

TACTFULNESS

One who loves men and understands them will usually have the quality of *tactfulness* and the faculty of putting others at their ease, but this is not always the case. In the selection of an employment supervisor this quality is definitely considered apart from any other. In order to judge men fairly and accurately in all respects one must study them when they are at ease and expressing themselves naturally and normally. It is the practice of some employers to summon applicants before them and then, assuming a fierce expression and harsh voice, to grill them unmercifully — a method which usually adds greatly to the employer's good opinion of himself and his pleasure in his own performances, but which is effective, too, in eliminating from consideration all but the most brazen and thick-skinned. That such applicants often turn out to be deceivers and trouble makers, and therefore the least desirable of all possible employees, is sufficient commentary on this method. Since it is the constructive thought and feeling of workers we desire, that employment supervisor is most efficient who most successfully inspires such thought and feeling in the employee from the moment he enters the institution to make application for work. Furthermore, it is by tactfulness that confidence is gained and harmonious relations begun.

TEACHABLENESS

Having satisfied ourselves that our prospective employment supervisor has these desirable intellectual and social qualities, we next consider his *teachableness*.

We have found it possible to accomplish almost anything with a man who has a pliable, youthful mind, no matter what his years, who has a broad outlook on life, and who never seems to forget that his sum of knowledge, be it little or great, is a mere atom in the mass of what may be learned. When we find a man who knows that new discoveries tomorrow may render obsolete the highest wisdom of to-day — especially his own — and who, therefore, is not only receptive of but eager for more and more truth, we are very hopeful of him, no matter what may be his other qualifications or lack of them. An employment supervisor works with human beings in whom there is constant variation. He is applying the principles of a comparatively new science to which additions are being made constantly. He is likely to find himself dealing with subordinates and associates who consider that they have learned all that can be learned about their business.

For all these reasons, it is highly important that an employment supervisor should not only be teachable, but that he should be the kind of man who will never lose this quality of teachableness.

JUDICIAL MIND

Sit for half a day in the office of a successful employment supervisor and you will be impressed with the essentially *judicial* quality of his *mind*.

First, there comes an applicant desiring work. The applicant presents to the best of his ability evidence of his fitness. In the candidate as he stands there, the keen eye of the employment supervisor sees elements of both fitness and unfitness; he sees certain qualities which would fit the applicant for one kind of work, and other qualities which would fit him for another. In addition to these considerations, there may be recommendations from former employers, or even from foremen or department heads in the organization who wish the man employed in their departments. And so there is presented in one form or another evidence for the man, and evidence against him.

The employment supervisor weighs the evidence, makes sure that he has not overlooked any of the points, that he has accurate and definite knowledge and not mere guesswork as his guide, that he gives to each consideration its due weight, but not too much weight, and that he reasons logically and soundly to his conclusion. He either sends the applicant to some foreman or head of department, with a recommendation, or tells him there is nothing for him and why there is nothing.

Fig. 21. C. F. Rumely. The first employment supervisor appointed under the Blackford Employment Plan

Next comes a gang-boss with one of his workers. They do not work peaceably together. The boss says he wants to give the man every chance to do his work and that he has exhausted his resources in attempting to arrive at a basis of mutual understanding and harmony with him. The workman says he wants to do his best and that he has tried to be efficient and loyal, but maintains that the boss is suspicious of him and unjust to him. The employment supervisor listens to them, one at a time, hears both sides without prejudice, and renders his decision.

Next comes a young man with a complaint against his immediate superior. The employment supervisor refuses to hear a word of it until he has summoned the executive, so that the statement can be made in his presence. By the time his superior arrives the complainant has about decided that he has nothing to say.

The employment supervisor makes it clear that he is always ready to listen to and will encourage frank statement and discussion of differences, but that he will not permit tattling and tale-bearing.

In any mass of evidence there will be some apparent contradictions. They are seldom real. By careful checking they can almost always be harmonized. A reliable judge will do this. The judicial mind, with its deliberate, sound judgment, valuable at many other places in the business, is perhaps most valuable in an employment supervisor.

KEEN OBSERVATION

As has already been pointed out, one of the most difficult lessons for the average person to learn with reference to human nature is that no one feature or indication is sufficient basis for reliable judgment. Everything about a man is significant of his character. No one thing tells the whole story, and the only way to be certain of correct judgment is to observe accurately and weigh carefully every indication. To do this one must have not only good judgment but keen observation. Other things being equal, we select for employment supervisors those who have the *keenest and most accurate powers of observation*.

Keenness of observation is partly inherent, but no matter what the natural endowments of a man, they must be painstakingly cultivated. And the way to cultivate powers of observation for an employment supervisor is by practice, practice, practice—always checking up and verifying deductions by subsequent behaviour of those selected.

The six requisites (understanding of human nature, sympathy, tactfulness, teachableness, a judicial mind, and keen observation) described in the foregoing are inherent, fundamental, and indispensable in any employment supervisor. They depend more upon natural endowment than upon education. We have found any man having them in goodly degree fairly well equipped for the position. To these qualifications, however, it is wise to add others by study and training. One of the most important of these is a *working knowledge of the essential qualities required for each class of work in the institution*. Employment supervisors working under our plan acquire this knowledge by careful study of duties, efficiencies, operations, and other factors, by taking counsel with foremen, heads of departments, and other executives, by consulting with efficiency experts as to the best way of doing each task and the requirements for doing it in that way.

WOMEN AS EMPLOYMENT SUPERVISORS

A careful consideration of these seven qualifications will perhaps suggest to the discriminating that women are especially fitted for the position of employment supervisor, and this we have found to be the case.

In one institution, a young woman who has these qualities in an unusual degree, with comparatively little instruction from us, has organized an employment department of which she is the supervisor. So resourceful and tactful has she been that she has won the hearty coöperation and support of the management, as well as the respect and confidence of their store managers, salesmen, heads of departments, foremen, and other employees. Another young woman, member of the staff of an employment supervisor, carried the entire responsibility for shop employment in an institution with 2,500 on the pay-roll. She was treated with the greatest respect and deference by even the roughest and coarsest labourers. More than any man in the department, she was able to gain their confidence. In many cases her ready sympathies and quick, womanly wit enabled her to adjust difficulties with which the men could not cope. In other cases the men brought to her personal and family troubles that were handicapping them in their work, and she was able, by the sound common sense of her advice, to suggest practical solutions which were often accepted. This young woman was able to administer discipline effectively. She could speak firmly and reprimand men in a way that would not have been tolerated from a foreman or superintendent, and it did them good.

Here, then, is a new field for women. Here also is a suggestion to employers for careful consideration when organizing employment departments.

The numerical strength of the employment supervisor's staff depends largely upon circumstances. In organizations employing only a few men, the employment supervisor himself does all the work, with the aid of a clerk and stenographer. He may even occupy some other position. In a small bank, the cashier performs the duties of employment supervisor. In some retail stores the proprietor himself does the work. In a large organization employing upward of 5,000 men, the employment supervisor has a staff of six. Of these, four interview applicants, attend to adjustments and transfers, standardize requirements for positions, and in general assist the employment supervisor in his dealings with employees. One handles the correspondence, and one takes care of the files and records.

SELECTION OF EXECUTIVES

In the actual work of interviewing it is customary for the employment supervisor himself to select and assign department heads and other important executives. In the selection of men for the highest positions in the organization he acts in an advisory capacity to the general manager, president, or board of directors, as the case may be. Perhaps none of his functions is more important than this of selecting executives and higher officials.

The executive sounds the keynote in his department, so that it becomes a reflection of his personality. Competent, efficient executives who think and feel constructively, and who inspire constructive thought and feeling may easily build up any business institution. It is a thankless and almost fruitless task to select a force of reliable and efficient workers in the lower ranks when those in official chairs are unreliable and inefficient. Too many employment supervisors have wasted their time and energy in trying to build up an ideal organization from the bottom. The place to begin is at the top.

Those employment supervisors are most successful who begin by securing the coöperation of the management, help to select executives and department heads who are efficient and trustworthy; then coöperate closely with them to build up the desired quality in the rank and file.

CHAPTER XII

SOME FUNCTIONS OF AN EMPLOYMENT DEPARTMENT

THE functions of an employment department vary according to the size, location, character, and organization of the institution in which it is installed. Some departments exercise a very wide range of functions, covering practically all relations between employer and employees. Others are more restricted in their scope. But there are certain functions common to all. These we shall discuss in this chapter.

RECOMMENDS FOR EMPLOYMENT

It is not the function of the employment department arbitrarily to employ and discharge help. It is important to bear in mind that the employment supervisor does not give orders to executives and their employees; that his function is to secure information, classify knowledge, and make recommendations for action.

The employment department, having determined just what kind of employees are wanted in the organization, makes use of its knowledge and equipment in securing the very best available people, analyzes and classifies these applicants scientifically, and recommends them for employment according to their fitness.

Human beings for the most part are easily led, and it is not hard to persuade them to accept competent assistants. It is exceedingly difficult, however, to drive them. The average executive is not only willing but glad to have a good man recommended to him by even a mediocre employment supervisor, but he rebels, and rightly, when he has men forced upon him, no matter how good they are or how expert the employment supervisor.

REASSIGNS AND READJUSTS

Rarely is it our privilege to install an employment department in a brand-new organization at the very inception of its work. That would be the ideal way, for then every worker in the organization would be scientifically chosen. In the great majority of cases, employment departments are installed in organizations where other methods have been in use for longer or shorter periods. The department, therefore, finds practically all positions filled when it begins its work. Some of these positions may be filled with competent and efficient men; others not.

It is a function of the employment department to make readjustments as rapidly as possible. Generally we find that most employees can be saved to the organization by transferring those who are misfits to places where they fit. As already indicated, it has been found best to make these transfers and readjustments gradually, and as occasion arises.

In handling human beings, under any conditions, the lessons of political, industrial, and commercial history teach plainly enough the truth that changes must be brought about by a process of evolution, rather than by a sweeping revolution, if best results are to be obtained at least expense.

The advantages gained by institutions and individuals as the result of this process of readjustment and transfer are sometimes very great. In one institution, for example, we found a superintendent of one of the factories who held his position because he was a brother-in-law of the general manager. Very soon after the department began its work there, the superintendent came in and requested an interview. In straightforward sincerity he confessed that, although his intentions were good, he was a failure as superintendent.

"My men think a lot of me," he said, "and would do anything for me. With such backing I ought to be making a star record. But I can't get details into my head. In spite of all I can do, I keep on making blunders — some of them pretty bad. I tell you, I am nervous and scared all the time for fear one of my mistakes may get somebody killed or blow up the shop. I'm in the wrong job as superintendent."

The man was absolutely right. He was splendidly qualified in many ways but had so little capacity for details that it would be hard to imagine a poorer choice for superintendent of a factory. At our suggestion he was transferred to the sales department, where he has made a gratifying record.

On one of our great railroads a young man who was marking time and making only mediocre success as stenographer in the traffic manager's office was transferred to the purchasing department. There he speedily proved his special aptitude for that kind of work. Within a comparatively few years, and while still very young, this former stenographer became purchasing agent not only for this railroad but for all associated lines. His superiors and associates tell us that he is without question one of the most efficient railway purchasing agents in the country.

In Cleveland, Ohio, we found a young man working as a common mechanic upon heavy, coarse machinery. He was discontented, unhappy, and

AN EMPLOYMENT DEPARTMENT

doing only just enough work to hold his job. In fact, his foreman was only waiting for a good opportunity to let him go. Seeing fine mechanical and executive ability in the young man, we recommended his transfer to a department where he could work on light machinery, with fine tools, and where an element of beauty entered into his work; also that he be made understudy to the foreman. The change was accordingly made, and as a result the young man awoke, became ambitious, threw himself heartily into his work, and astonished his superiors. To-day he is part owner and general manager of a prosperous automobile factory.

In every institution where ordinary methods of employment have been used there will be found some employees who are either unfit for any class of work in that particular institution or, because of serious mental, moral, or physical deficiencies, utterly unfit for employment in any capacity. It is the function of an employment department to eliminate such people from the organization as rapidly and with as little friction and trouble as possible. For those who might be good assets in a concern doing some other kind of work it is often easy to find openings. A well-conducted and successful employment department soon becomes known to other business concerns. Letters and telegrams from them are constantly coming in asking for reliable men who perhaps do not fit in the organization where the employment department is, but who would be valuable in some other line of business.

HANDLES MISFITS

Building up an ideal organization is slow work. Indeed, since every organization must be composed of faulty and imperfect human beings, the ideal is always just out of reach. It is never possible to fill every position with the man who has all the standard requirements, or to eliminate from the organization all undesirables. Besides, there is no profit in discharging an unfit employee only to fill his place with one equally or even more unfit. We have sometimes retained men in important positions long after it had been decided to remove them, while we were looking for just the right men to fill their places. The need in all such cases is to shift undesirables to positions where they will be least objectionable and to place them under such restrictions and supervision as will leave them with the least opportunity for doing harm.

PROVIDES UNDERSTUDIES

Human affairs are subject to change. Even the best and seemingly the most reliable executive or other employee may die or resign or be promoted.

In such cases employers often find themselves greatly embarrassed. The more valuable the employee, as a general rule, the more difficult it is to find a successor. While the place is vacant, oftentimes the employer suffers serious loss.

It is the function of an employment department to provide against such emergencies. The best way to do this, from every point of view, is to see that every important employee in the organization has a competent understudy.

There is always less friction in making a change when a man is promoted from within the organization. Such a man understands the policies, the traditions, the ideals, and the methods of the house. He knows and understands his associates, subordinates, and superiors. If he has been an understudy, he understands the duties of the particular position to which he is promoted and assumes them without delay, without an expensive period of "learning the ropes," and without a moment's groping takes hold of obscure but important details of the position.

The effect upon the spirit of other employees is important. "I wish you would tell me what is the matter with my men," one employer said to us. "They are well paid. Their hours of labour are short. I do my best to treat them kindly and considerately. And yet they are discontented, ungrateful, and most of the time almost in a state of mutiny. What is the trouble?"

It required only a short investigation to find the trouble. On three different occasions within a year some important and desirable position had become vacant. On each occasion the men expected that one of their own number would be promoted. Notwithstanding his good intentions, and notwithstanding the fact that he had men in his own organization who could have filled the positions creditably, this short-sighted manager had brought in people from the outside.

In contrast with this is the case of an organization where we did some work. Here we found that every man in an important executive or staff position had been promoted from the ranks, and that in twenty years only one man had been brought in from the outside to fill a position of authority and responsibility.

It used to be a very common thing for employers to hire stars away from other organizations by offering them fabulous salaries. This practice has fallen more and more into disuse as one after another of these high-priced acquisitions has proved to be a losing investment. While other managers are purchasing star players from other teams at from five to twenty thousand dollars each, and then paying them big salaries, "Connie Mack" (Cornelius McGillicuddy) chooses his players from among college boys and amateurs. He doesn't pay a cent for their release, and they are only too glad to start in at moderate salaries. But Connie Mack knows men. He can see in a young man the aptitudes which, with proper training, will make him a world's champion pitcher or catcher, and he knows how to give that kind of training.

SECURES DESIRABLE APPLICANTS

Just as Connie Mack and other successful baseball managers have their scouts scouring the country for promising material, so an efficient employment department is always alert and aggressively seeking desirable men, principally within the organization, but in general wherever they are likely to be found. These prospective captains, managers, and generals are analyzed, their abilities are carefully studied, and the analysis, together with other useful information, is kept for reference in the files of the employment department. The longer such a list is and the more carefully it is kept, the more valuable it becomes.

KEEPS RELIABLE AND ADEQUATE RECORDS

One of the most important of all the functions of an employment department is the keeping of records. The spirit of the age is scientific. Conclusions are based not upon personal opinion, not upon hearsay, not upon mere guesses or estimates, but upon accurate and reliable exact knowledge.

What does it cost to operate an employment department? Its records show. What is the financial benefit to the organization of an employment department? The records give the answer. What is the value of this man? Should he be transferred, or promoted, or demoted, or discharged? What is his record? What has been his performance, his deportment? What is the value of this executive's opinion of his men? His opinions are recorded and on the same record are shown the actual performances of his men. How do they agree? How accurately do the employment supervisor and members of his staff analyze applicants, and how wisely do they select, assign, and transfer employees? Here are their analyses in the records, and here are the showings of the employees. How do they compare? What percentage of employees selected by the employment department prove to be well fitted for their positions and efficient in them? Consult the records.

The records of the employment department are thus a guide for the future work of the department and a reliable measure of its efficiency. They afford a scientific basis for dealing with each employee. They show the trend of the whole organization.

AN EMPLOYMENT DEPARTMENT

They are a valuable source of study to the employment supervisor and his staff, ripening and perfecting their understanding and practical application of the principles upon which employees are analyzed. If desired, the general manager and other executives may have on their desks, daily, weekly, or monthly, a report showing the number of employees hired, promoted, transferred, or increased in compensation during the period covered, together with such other information as occasion requires. In this way they may keep fully informed regarding the employment situation.

ADJUSTS DIFFERENCES AND HEARS COMPLAINTS

Every employee is given to understand that he may come freely to the employment department and state his grievances, if he has any, and that every case of inefficiency, discontent, inharmony, and misunderstanding will be decided only upon the evidence and always with a desire to be just.

In an institution where an employment department had been installed, a foreman noticed that one of his best workers was becoming careless. The man, who had always been accurate and reliable, committed one blunder after another. Day by day these became more frequent and more exasperating. He remonstrated with the man, at first kindly, then more sharply, but the man did not improve. Then the foreman warned him two or three times, and finally returned him to the employment department. The department investigated and found that the man's wife had been ill for many weeks, and that he had been losing sleep while he sat up and nursed her night after night. He was reprimanded for not reporting the case to the employment department at the beginning. The company's nurse was sent to the home and the man given a vacation on full pay to recuperate. In a few days the man returned to work with his former efficiency. Thus a valuable asset was saved to the company and the psychical effect, not only upon this one man but his fellow-workers, was worth many times the cost. This incident illustrates one of the most important functions of an employment department—namely, the care of the health of employees.

GIVES MEDICAL EXAMINATIONS — SUPERVISES SANITATION

In every department there is a medical division under the direction of a competent physician, who gives either all or part of his time according to the size of the institution and character of work done. It is the duty of this physician, when called upon, to examine applicants before they are finally recom-

AN EMPLOYMENT DEPARTMENT

mended. The department maintains such emergency and other hospitals as may be needed; keeps close supervision over the health of all employees and over sanitation in the offices, factories, and stores of the concern; and also in the homes of employees; supplies competent nurses, who are often far more important than physicians, and gives instruction to all employees in regard to hygiene and sanitation.

SUPERVISES "WELFARE WORK"

Night schools, training classes, apprentice schools, musical, literary, and athletic clubs within the organization; lunch rooms, rest rooms, entertainments, dances, games, sports, safety, insurance, loans, pensions, and all other such features of what is known as welfare work or social betterment among employees are most efficiently cared for by the employment department. When a department is organized under the direction and supervision of a properly selected and trained employment supervisor, all these activities are left to his discretion.

In short, it is the function of the employment department to compile all necessary data and, working from these data as a basis, to do everything possible to build up an ideal organization such as we have pictured in Chapter II.

SEEKS COÖPERATION OF MANAGEMENT

In all its functions the employment department proceeds with the knowledge that it cannot stand alone. To be successful it must have the support and hearty coöperation of the management and of every other department in the organization. Its work must be made a definite part of the policy of the concern. This, as we have before indicated, is sometimes one of the hardest tasks the employment department has to perform.

It often happens that some department head has excellent reasons of his own for opposing the use of scientific methods. In one case where we were installing an employment department, an important official refused to coöperate with us, would not even see us, blustered and slammed his receiver up in our face when we tried to talk to him over the telephone. Afterward we met the gentleman quite by accident and had an opportunity to look him over. It was immediately and abundantly clear why he had violently resisted the presence on the general manager's staff of any one who was reputed to be able to read character. In the ordinary course of business, a few weeks later, we were requested to report upon a number of executives in the organization. This man's name was on the list. We were obliged to advise an immediate investigation of his department. The investigation

AN EMPLOYMENT DEPARTMENT

followed, and such serious inefficiencies and irregularities were found that the organization was speedily relieved of this executive.

It is not always necessary, however, to take such drastic action.

Securing the coöperation of the management of any institution is frequently difficult but seldom impossible. However, it requires patience, tact, courage, good nature, persistence, and, above all, a true and genuine desire to render service to the organization. In many cases the employment department has received the sincere and enthusiastic coöperation of the management from the very beginning. In such cases the work is a pleasure, and the results obtained more than justify our most sanguine expectations for the application of scientific methods to employment.

CHAPTER XIII

THE ART OF HANDLING MEN

THERE are two distinct factors in the successful handling of men: First, the boss, or executive; second, the workers, or subordinates.

SELF-MASTERY

No man can ever hope successfully to handle other men who cannot first master himself.

Some examples will illustrate:

There is a type of man who is often found in a position where he has charge of others who is himself personally inefficient. He is careless. He is thoughtless. He is hot-headed and emotional. He constantly makes errors. He loses and mislays things. He procrastinates. And for all these inefficiencies he holds himself blameless and shoulders the responsibility upon his subordinates. No one ever knows where to find him or how to please him. He is as whimsical as a spoiled child. When pleased he is honeyed of speech and extravagant in praise. When displeased he is erratic, unjust, and vindictive. He makes promises lightly which perhaps at the moment he expects to fulfil. But he quickly forgets them. This man and every one with whom he comes in contact are at the mercy of his emotions. His intellect, will, and sense of justice are all subordinate to the way he "feels."

Another type is the self-centred man who measures every one by his own erroneous conception of himself. In a position of authority he sets himself up to be adored and worshipped. He is extremely jealous of his authority, wants to "know it all," and resents suggestions from any one, probably fearing that to accept them will lower him in the estimation of others. This man is usually prejudiced, narrow, and bigoted, and in dealing with others assumes a patronizing air. In rendering decisions he is apt to show the most unexpected pettiness.

Another, unsuccessful in the highest meaning of the term, is the unsympathetic, harsh, exacting, unforgiving, relentless man who attempts to rule others by fear. Fear, like brute strength, is one of the crudest weapons possessed by mankind. Fear always engenders hatred. So the man who is feared invariably has the hatred and contempt of others.

None of these types is successful in handling men. There are many others, and some of them no doubt will be suggested by those we have described.

There are certain qualities of character which appeal to all mankind. The individual who possesses them can handle others without difficulty.

SENSE OF JUSTICE

At the head of the list we place *a keen sense of justice*. In the broad sense of the term, a sense of justice includes honesty, the disposition to give the square deal, integrity, truthfulness, and the ability to weigh all the evidence before rendering a decision. No matter how untruthful and dishonest a man may be, he invariably respects one who is truthful and just.

A young man was once heard to remark as he was leaving his superior's office, "He is the whitest man I ever knew." "Why?" inquired one of his associates. "Did he reinstate you?" "Reinstate me? No, he fired me. But he talked to me like a father."

DEPENDABLENESS

Scarcely less indispensable than a keen sense of justice is the quality of *dependableness*, steadfastness, or constancy. In speaking of his chief, a man once said: "He is the most dependable man I have ever known. Day after day, no matter what the circumstances, he is the same considerate and gentlemanly fellow that you see to-day. He never makes promises that he does not keep, and in all the years I have worked for him I have never known him to lose his temper." Perhaps no quality in an executive gives greater confidence to his subordinates than to know that when he appears in the morning he will greet them with a pleasant and responsive smile, and that under all circumstances they will know exactly what to expect from him.

COURAGE

Successful dealing with others sometimes requires great courage. It takes courage to administer rebuke even when the offender richly deserves it. It takes courage to refrain from being extravagant in one's praise when some kindly act has been directed toward one's self. But perhaps courage is required most of all to admit that one is wrong. And so, third on our list of desirable qualities of character, we place courage.

SYMPATHY AND LOVE

Even the most unresponsive and callous individual is mellowed when convinced that you are genuinely interested in him and his welfare. The quality of human sympathy is indispensable in dealing with others. We often criticise others harshly and unjustly, largely because we are unable to put ourselves in their place. One of the cardinal principles in salesmanship is to secure the name of the customer and remember it so as to address him by name when next you meet him. This is only one indirect way of showing the quality of friendly interest and sympathy.

Very closely akin to sympathy is the quality of love. One almost hesitates to use the term, so greatly has it been misused. There is a sloppy sentimentality current among some types of business men which is pure affectation. Its use is greatly to be deplored. Even an animal knows whether or not you are fond of it. We know a sociable little kitten who looks over every guest that comes into the house, and never once has she committed the blunder of making overtures to any one who does not like cats. One is naturally drawn to those who have in their hearts a sincere love of humanity and who express that love, not in extravagant and endearing terms, but in acts of genuine kindness and affection.

During a strike on a street railway line, one of the officials, who had temporarily taken up his residence in a downtown hotel, observed that one of his Irish foremen was also stopping at the same place, and no matter where the official went it seemed that big Mike was always near him. After a few days he said to the man: "Mike, I know that your salary isn't big enough for you to afford to live at this hotel. What are you doing here, anyway?" By means of considerable questioning he persuaded Mike to confess: "Well, sir, ye see thim Dagos threatened to git ye and I thought I'd better be handy." That incident happened many years ago, but even to-day this official cannot mention Michael Flaherty without a mist in his eyes.

TACTFULNESS

We have known men to possess all of the desirable qualities we have mentioned and yet fail of the greatest success because they lacked the tactfulness necessary to handle a difficult situation. There are those who are so dynamic that their words are like sledge-hammer blows, and when with the best intentions they administer a reprimand they are often surprised to find that they have utterly paralyzed the activities of their workers. It requires both courtesy and tactfulness to deal successfully with others.

TEACHABLENESS

Our list of desirable human qualities would be far from complete if we omitted teachableness. There is none so wise but that he may learn from others. We have known many executives who were not above the average in ability who scored great successes because they were open-minded and had the happy faculty of securing suggestions of value from their workers.

UNDERSTANDING OF PEOPLE

Supplement the foregoing human qualities with an understanding of character and you have the man who can handle others. An efficiency expert made up from time studies a schedule for a given workman. He went to his worker and explained to him that he had made up a very easy schedule, allowing twenty-four minutes in which to complete each piece. Said he: "Now you can make one in twenty-four minutes or you can beat it," meaning of course that he could easily make the piece in less than the allotted time. The workman received the explanation in silence, and a few minutes after the efficiency man had gone he went to his foreman and asked for his time. "But why are you quitting?" insisted the foreman. "Well, you know that efficiency man. He came around a little while ago and said that I could either make a pinion every twenty-four minutes or get-to-hell out of here." This incident is significant. More inharmony and friction between men result from misunderstanding than from any other one cause.

Each individual is in many respects like others,

THE ART OF HANDLING MEN 247

and a general policy or a given attitude will, in a measure, fit all; but each individual also has his peculiarities and in some particulars is different from every one else. So the man who expects to deal with all men in the same manner cannot hope to be more than a partial success.

There is a type of man who is wholly unable to reason logically. He reaches his conclusions by intuition and decides every question in the light of self-interest. He is found among all grades of men, from the lowest to the highest. We have seen executives waste hours trying to reason this type out of his decision and then grow furiously angry when the man failed to respond. Understanding of the man alone will save one the humiliation of expecting from another what he is unable to give. We do not grow angry when a deaf man fails to hear us. We observe his infirmity and take different measures from sound to communicate with him. When a man lacks the power of reason or lacks any other human trait, we should observe his deficiency and use measures in dealing with him that do not require the exercise of the deficient faculty.

There are many other human traits that are admirable and lovable that go to make up the all-around, well-developed man, and which contribute to success. But the man who possesses in strong degree a keen sense of justice, dependableness, courage, sympathy, love, tactfulness, courtesy, teachableness, and an understanding of human nature, will be more than an ordinary success.

CHAPTER XIV

EDUCATING EMPLOYEES

IT IS characteristic of an age of machinery that the average employer of yesterday should regard his employees largely as fixed values, capable perhaps of some increase in efficiency through improved methods, but fundamentally unchangeable and unchanging until they begin to wear out. If the employer of large numbers of men was conscious of the fact that they were capable of growth and development, he gave very little evidence of this consciousness until recently.

We have known employers who paid $10,000 a year to an expert to train their horses, or $5,000 a year to a dog trainer, but not one cent for the training and education of the men and women upon whose ability and efficiency they depended for success in business. We have heard the heads of corporations complain bitterly that it was impossible to find men capable of filling their ten, fifteen, and thirty thousand dollar a year positions. Yet these same corporations have had thousands of men in their employ for more than a quarter of a century, and have left their development into extraordinary ability wholly to chance. So obsessed are some otherwise intelligent employers by the machine idea of man that we have seen them resist stubbornly a proposition to invest so little a sum as $25 each in the education of a picked class of their employees, and this when the employees were sufficiently interested and ambitious to be willing to invest $25 each of their own money in the tuition. We have seen employers reluctantly consent to spend a few dollars on the organization of a class for study of some special educational feature; then turn over the class to the employees themselves, giving nothing of their moral support and personal attention to the success of the venture. This is the type of employer who afterward insists against all argument that it is a waste of money to establish classes for employees — he has tried it and he knows.

BUSINESS INSTITUTIONS AS SCHOOLS

With the rapid growth of industry, with the unprecedented increase in the size of our manufacturing and commercial institutions, and in the number of men employed, with the excessive emphasis which has been placed upon machinery and other equipment, upon methods and system, it is not surprising that employers have overlooked the

EDUCATING EMPLOYEES

fact that in their employees they have unguessed resources of mental and psychical wealth-producing power waiting only for development. It is not surprising that they have until very recently failed to grasp the possibilities for development of individual capabilities in the relationship between employer and employee. Certain great minds have perceived this truth in comparatively recent years. Educational work done in the institutions they dominate has demonstrated that not even in our best schools and colleges have we so effective an opportunity for education as in our commercial and industrial institutions.

It is the modern idea in education that we learn best by doing, that there is greater development of better quality achieved through the intelligently guided and instructed work of the hands than through the study of books or listening to lectures alone. This is one principle underlying the Montesorri Method, manual training, vocational training, farm and industrial schools, and other of the newer methods of education which have been found successful.

Many employers not only fail to avail themselves of the possibilities of growth in their employees by means of special classes, but utterly neglect the benefits to be derived from instruction of the employee in connection with his own work. For example, in one institution coming under our notice, the sixty-five foremen were ordered to install and apply the bonus system of compensation to employees. When the attempt to enforce this order failed it was found that sixty-two out of the sixty-five foremen did not know what the bonus system was, much less what were its workings and results. While it is not always possible or desirable to enlighten employees as to the "inside" reasons for issuing certain orders and adopting certain policies, as a general rule people do far better work when they know just what they are doing and why. The effect of a very little kindly instruction in this respect has often proved remarkable.

"MAN OR MACHINE — WHICH?"

A careless pipe-fitter was returned to the employment department by his foreman. He had been "called" and warned repeatedly, but still his work was unreliable, and now he was sent back to the employment department for discharge. The employment supervisor talked with the man, asked him a few questions, and learned that he had little conception of the purpose and importance of the work entrusted to him. His foreman was called in and both men were given a vivid word picture of what happened, perhaps a thousand miles away from the factory, when pipe-fitting was defective

EDUCATING EMPLOYEES

in the company's product. Not only did the workman go back to his work with an inspiration that made him more accurate and careful thereafter, but the foreman, with this object lesson before him, by the same kind of careful instruction improved the efficiency of several others in his department.

In this same factory, the employment supervisor encountered a man who had been working for twenty years making one small part, not knowing where it fitted into the finished product. It may be true, as some critics have observed, that the man was lacking in imagination and initiative or he would have taken the pains to learn for himself. And yet that his employer was even more to blame is evidenced by the fact that when the fascinating story of that little piece of machinery was told by the employment supervisor the old man almost wept with emotion, and thereafter what had been dull routine work became almost a religious rite with him.

Stand a man before a machine ten hours a day, simply feeding in material, turning handles, and pulling levers. The work requires no thought, no particular skill, no originality, no initiative. There are certain definite movements for the man's hands, just as there are for the cogs and levers of the machine. As he stands there day after day, the man feels that he is but a slave of the machine, that tomorrow some inventor may design an attachment that will do his work more swiftly and more accurately than he. The machine will eventually wear out and be tossed upon the scrap-heap. The man knows that he, too, will eventually wear out and be tossed upon the scrap-heap. Is it strange that so many feel that they are slaves to the machine and grow discontented, embittered, and ready for riot or revolution? But let that man's employer educate him to understand the machine and its processes, so that he can devote his thought, his originality, his initiative to the improvement of that machine or to the invention of a new one that will displace it altogether, and what a different point of view he has. He is no longer slave but master of the machine. He rises superior to it, because by the exercise of thought he can improve or even replace it. This thought is developed in a masterly way by Al Priddy in his book, "Man or Machine — Which?"

Institutions where employees are thus educated and where suggestions from them are made welcome and, when found worthy, are rewarded, have profited greatly by reason of improvements suggested by employees. But they have profited even more by the psychical and educational effect of the sense of mastery thus produced.

EDUCATING EMPLOYEES

We have already mentioned the great and too often unused educational and inspirational value of the history, policies, traditions, and ideals of the organization. An efficient employment department never loses sight of the truth, in every phase of its work, that its supreme duty is to secure for the institution, not the large bones and muscles and weight-lifting strength of men, but their highest and best constructive thought and feeling.

ADAPTING EDUCATION TO THE INDIVIDUAL

In educational circles we are hearing more and more of the cry that instruction must be adapted to the individual. We are learning that it is wasteful and inefficient to put every child through the same ironclad routine of school work. The principle is sound, and is nowhere more thoroughly understood than in an employment department organized upon the basis of the plan we are presenting. Supplementing education of the general character already suggested in this chapter and in special night and day classes of various kinds, the employment department instructs each employee upon two very important phases of his relationship to the organization. First, each employee receives careful instruction as to the standard requirements of his particular position. His duties are definitely outlined for him, and the qualifications he must possess and develop for their most efficient performance are stated. He is given specific instruction as to his own mental and physical equipment with reference to these qualifications, and how he may develop and improve it. In various ways, according to his type, he is encouraged and stimulated to live up to the standard set for him. Second, he is carefully taught what line of promotion will best fit his particular case and how best to fit himself to grow into more and more responsible and better paid service.

In general, it is the purpose of the department to give every man work that will keep him stretching upward to do it — a job just a little bigger than he is; so that he has before him always an incentive to grow up to his opportunities. Fear of punishment must frequently be used, no doubt, to drive a man out of the depths, but only hope of reward can lead him up to the heights.

There is no greater natural resource than the latent intellectual and psychical force of our people. Largely because we have left the development of these possibilities to chance or to charity, we struggle to-day against an incredible inertia of inefficiency. Because we have left these fertile fields to grow up to weeds or to be cultivated by the ignorant or the designing, we are sometimes frightened when we awake to the menace of a harvest of class struggle and revolution. Only through wise and scientific education and development of our workers shall we overcome these threatening tendencies in our body politic, and begin to utilize for ourselves and for the race the unmeasured latent aptitudes of man applied intelligently to the infinite resources of the universe.

CHAPTER XV

VOCATIONAL GUIDANCE

THE problem of better methods of employment and more harmonious relationship between employer and employee is of such acute and immediate importance that it takes form in the minds of many thoughtful people as an imminent crisis in human affairs. And yet it is only a part of a still broader and still more insistent problem. A very great deal of the mischief of unfitness of man for his job is done before the young person presents himself for employment. Parents and teachers, groping in the dark, have long been training natural born artists to become mechanics, natural born business men to become musicians, and boys and girls with great aptitudes for agriculture and horticulture to become college professors, lawyers, and doctors.

The waste of splendid human talent, amounting in some cases to positive genius, as a result of the obstinacy of parents, the out-of-date traditionalism of our schools, and the utter ignorance of both, is distressing. In our experience, covering a dozen years of careful investigation and the examination of many thousands of individuals, we have seen so much of the tragedy of the misfit that it seems at times almost universal. The records of one thousand persons taken at random from our files show that 763, or 76.3 per cent., felt that they were in the wrong vocations. Of these 414 were thirty-five years old or older. Most of these, when questioned as to why they had entered upon occupations for which they had so little natural aptitude, stated that they had either drifted along lines of least resistance or had been badly advised by parents, teachers, or employers.

HOW TALENT GOES TO WASTE

We knew a wealthy father, deaf to all pleas from his children, who spent thousands of dollars upon what he thought was a musical education for his daughter, including several years in Europe. The young lady could not become a musician. The aptitude for music was not in her. But she was unusually talented in mathematics and appreciation of financial values, and could have made a marked success had she been permitted to gratify her constantly reiterated desire for a commercial career. This same father, with the same obstinacy, insisted that his son go into business. The young man was so passionately determined to make a career of music that he was a complete failure in business and finally embezzled several thousand dollars from his employer in the hope of making his escape to Europe and securing a musical education. Here were two human lives of marked talent hopelessly ruined and wasted by a well-intentioned but ignorant and obstinate parent.

A few years ago a young man was brought to us by his friends for advice. He had been educated for the law and then inherited from his father a considerable sum of money. Having no taste for the law and a repugnance for anything like office work, he had never even attempted to begin practice. Having nothing definite to do, he was becoming more and more dissipated, and when we saw him first had lost confidence in himself and was utterly discouraged. "I am useless in the world," he told us. "There is nothing I can do." At our suggestion, he was finally encouraged to purchase land and begin the scientific study and practice of horticulture. The last time we saw him he was erect, ruddy, hard-muscled, and capable looking. Best of all, his old, petulant, dissatisfied expression was gone. In its place was the light of worthy achievement, success, and happiness. He told us there were no finer fruit trees anywhere than his. Such incidents as this are not rare — indeed, they are commonplace. We could recount them from our records in great number. But every observant reader can supply many from his own experience.

THE VOCATIONAL MOVEMENT

It is a crime that thousands of young men and women should be encouraged, every year, to enroll in schools where they will spend time and money preparing themselves for professions already overcrowded and for which a large majority of them have no natural aptitudes. A prominent physician tells us that of the forty-eight who were graduated from medical school with him, he considers only three safe to consult upon medical subjects. Indeed, so great is the need and so increasingly serious is it becoming, as our industrial and commercial life grows more complex and the demand for conservation and efficiency more exacting, that progressive men and women in our universities and schools and elsewhere have undertaken a study of the vocational problem and are earnestly working toward a solution of it in vocational bureaus, vocational schools, and other ways, all together comprising the vocational movement.

Roger W. Babson, in his book, "The Future of the Working Classes: Economic Facts for Employers and Wage Earners," says: "The crowning work of an economic educational system will be vocational guidance. One of the greatest handicaps to all classes to-day is that 90 per cent. of the people have entered their present employment blindly and by chance, irrespective of their fitness or opportunities. Of course, the law of supply and demand is continually correcting these errors; but this readjusting causes most of the world's disappointments and losses. Some day the schools of the nation will be organized into a great reporting bureau on employment opportunities and trade conditions, directing the youths of the nation — so far as their qualifications warrant — into lines of work which then offer the greatest opportunity. Only by such a system will each worker receive the greatest income possible for himself, and also the greatest benefits possible from the labours of all, thus continually increasing production and yet avoiding overproduction in any single line." That the main features of the system suggested by Mr. Babson are being made the basis of the vocational movement is one of the most hopeful signs of the times.

FACTORS OF THE VOCATIONAL PROBLEM

The vocational problem consists: first, of the need of accurate vocational analysis; second, of the need of wise vocational counsel; third, of the need of adequate vocational training; fourth, of the need of correct vocational placement.

It is obvious that the vocational problem cannot be adequately solved by dealing with pupils or clients in groups or classes. It is a definite, specific, and individual problem. Group study is interesting and instructive, but alone does not give sufficient knowledge of individual peculiarities and aptitudes. It is obvious from the foregoing analysis of the vocational problem that it is practically identical at all points with the problem of scientific employment. Just as the highest efficiency of the employment department depends upon accurate analysis of the job and of the man, so the highest usefulness of the vocational bureau or vocational expert depends upon complete and exact knowledge of the requirements in different lines of endeavour, and the ability to analyze human nature accurately. It is obvious that wise counsel cannot be given, adequate training cannot be prescribed, and correct placement is impossible until these analyses have been properly made.

The child or adult of unusual ability, with well-marked inclinations, and strong in the fundamentals of character, is never difficult to analyze, counsel, train, or place. If given an opportunity to gain knowledge and freedom in the exercise of choice, he will almost surely gravitate into his natural line of work. He is not the real problem of the vocational expert. But the vast majority of children are average or even mediocre. They show little inclination toward any study or any work. They have weaknesses of character that will inevitably handicap them no matter what vocation they enter. They are the real problem. There is another class, almost equally distressing. They are the people who are brilliant, who learn easily, and who are so adaptable that they can turn their hands to almost anything. They are usually so unstable in temperament that it is difficult for them to persist in any one kind of endeavour long enough to score a success.

METHODS OF ANALYSIS IN USE

The need, in dealing with these problems, for some more reliable guide than the young person's inclinations and preferences has deeply impressed itself upon those engaged in vocational study and vocational work. They are earnestly seeking to find or to develop some better way. To this end, we have the questionaire, by which it is thought to bring out between the lines, as it were, the particular aptitudes and disposition of the subject. And this method is not without its advantages. We have also psychological tests. These are of fascinating interest and have yielded some valuable results. Some vocational workers use the psychological tests and some do not. Even those who are most enthusiastic for them admit that they are complicated, that they require expensive apparatus and specially trained examiners, and that even the best results obtainable cover a very narrow field in the character and aptitudes of the subject.

KIND OF METHOD NEEDED

The present need is for some uniform, readily applicable, inexpensive, and comprehensive method of analysis. The advantages of such a method are immediately apparent: First, its uniformity would permit the making of records for comparison, covering a very wide range of subjects, environment, and vocations. Second, even the simplest classifications which are readily learned and easily applied by the inexpert would yield tangible and measurable results and would be far better than the present unstandardized and wholly unscientific methods. Third, were such a uniform method adopted and made a part of the vocational work of our Y. M. C. A.'s, our social settlements, our public schools, our colleges and universities, and other institutions; were uniform records to be made and every subject analyzed, followed up, and his career studied, we should within one generation have data from which any intelligent, analytical mind could formulate a science of human analysis very nearly approaching exactitude. Fourth, as the result of the application of such a uniform method, the principles of human analysis would rapidly become a matter of common knowledge and could be taught in our schools just as we to-day teach the principles of chemical, botanical, or zoölogical analysis.

In the industries the scientific selection, assignment, and management of men have yielded increases in efficiency from 100 to 1,000 per cent. The majority of people thus dealt with were mature, with more or less fixity of character and habits. Many of them were handicapped by ironclad limitations and restrictions in their affairs and in their environment. What results may be possible when these methods, improved and developed by a wider use, are applied to children, with their plastic minds and wonderful latent possibilities, we cannot even venture to forecast.

THE END.

THE COUNTRY LIFE PRESS
GARDEN CITY, N. Y.